# Every Cloud has its Own Name

## Selected Poems and Essays of
## Cai Tianxin

Translated by
Robert Berold and Cai Tianxin

with additional translations by Sudeep Sen,
John Rosenwald, James Booze, Michelle Haight, Kuo-ch'ing Tu,
Robert Backus, Duncan James Poupard,
Xiujie Ma, and Patricia Nolan

1 Plus Books
San Francisco, 2017

# 每一片云都有它的名字

## 蔡天新 诗文集

罗伯特·贝洛尔德、蔡天新 译

部分诗作由苏迪普·森、约翰·罗森博格、
詹姆斯·布泽、米歇尔·哈特、杜国清、
罗伯特·巴库斯、邓肯·詹姆斯·普帕尔、
马秀杰和帕特丽西娅·诺兰翻译

壹嘉出版

旧金山·2017

# Contents

**I   In the ocean of the world**

In the ocean of the world /3
Sunlight /5
When summer retreats to the south along the
    wandering coastline /7
Stroll /9
From higher up /11
Division /13
Poem about fish /15
Trees and Dogs /17
Lake water /19
How to ask time to stay /21
Dream of living in the world /23

## II  The small boat of your nose

Poem /27
Flower /29
Naked /31
The river of my mind /33
The bench /35
Green wind /37
Lotus Lake /39
The number and the rose /41
Descartes /43
Overnight boat /45
Echo /47


## III  The highest pleasure

Wandering /51
Ancient road /53
Niagara Falls /55
The waves of Chennai /57
Palm trees /59
Explosion /61
The Erburz mountains /63
Trickle /65
The reading /67
Flight /69
The highest pleasure /71

## IV   Green blood

Green blood /75
Lake /77
Baoshi Hill /81
The beauty of my hometown /83
Wings of recollection /85
Hide and seek /87
Country girl receding on a covered tractor /89
Query /91
The persistence of memory /93
Skipping /95
At the water's edge /97


## V   Americas

Lake Titicaca /101
La Paz /103
Cuzco /105
The Great Wall /107
Golden Gate Bridge /109
On the way to Santa Barbara /111
Bowery Poetry Club /113
Boston /115
Harvard Square /117
Quebec /119
Vancouver /121

## VI  Far and near

Distant places /125
South Indian Garden /127
Octave Strait /129
From Moscow to St Petersburg Lake Geneva /131
Lake Geneva /133
Trois-Rivières /135
Far and near /137
Sleeping and writing /139
Qinghai Lake /141
When winter comes /143
Variation on a winter's Day /145

## VII  The heart of a poet

Every cloud has its own name /151
Poems are born from anxiety /153
The heart of a poet /155
The book of time /157
Cemetery /159
Soul /161
Deaths /163
Tribute to the victims /165
Avalanche /167
Difference /169
The Sky /171

## VIII  Song of the quiet life

1. Angel's breakfast /175
2. Missing Chopin /177
3. Song /179
4. Everything /181
5. Anxious trees /183
6. Flowering bones /185
7. Small bedroom /187
8. Life after noon /189
9. Body with many hands /191
10. Years of scattered stones /193
11. Wet silence /195
12. Elongated body /197
13. Night /199
14. Dark fruit /201
15. Fish /203
16. Bridge of the moon /205
17. Already too late /207
18. Song of the quiet life /209

## Appendix: Essays

West Lake /212
Mathematicians and poets /224

## Afterword by Robert Berold /233

# 目录

## I 世界的海洋

我们在世界的海洋上游泳 /2
阳光 /4
当盛夏沿着蜿蜒的海岸南移 /6
散步 /8
再远一点 /10
分割 /12
关于鱼的诗 /14
树木和狗 /16
湖水 /18
如何才能把时间挽留 /20
梦想活在世上 /22

## II 女人之花

诗 /26
女人之花 /28
裸体 /30
心灵的水面 /32
长椅 /34
绿风 /36
芙蓉湖 /38
数字和玫瑰 /40
笛卡尔 /42
夜航 /44
回声 /46

## III 最高乐趣

漫游 /50
罗马古道 /52
尼亚加拉瀑布 /54
夏奈的海浪 /56
棕榈 /58
爆炸 /60
厄尔布尔士山 /62
细流 /64
朗诵 /66
飞行 /68
最高乐趣 /70

## IV 绿血

绿血 /74
湖 /76
宝石山 /80
故乡的美人 /82
回想之翼 /84
橡皮 /86
村姑在有篷盖的拖拉机里远去 /88
疑问 /90
保留的记忆 /92
跳绳 /94
在水边 /36

## V 美洲

的的喀喀湖 /100
拉巴斯 /102
库斯科 /104
长城 /106
金门大桥 /108
去往圣芭芭拉路上 /110
　　——给张益唐
博厄里俱乐部 /112
波士顿 /114
哈佛广场 /116
魁北克 /118
温哥华 /120

## VI 远与近

远方 /124
南印度花园 /126
八度海峡 /128
从莫斯科到圣彼得堡 /130
日内瓦湖 /132
三河城 /134
远和近 /136
睡眠与写作 /138
青海湖 /140
冬天到来的时候 /142
冬日的变奏 /144

## VII 诗人的心

每一片云都有它的名字 /150
诗歌来源于焦虑 /152
诗人的心 /154
时间之书 /156
墓地 /158
心灵 /160
死亡 /162
为高铁事故遇难者而作 /164
雪崩 /166
差异 /168

## VIII　幽居之歌

1　天使的早点 /174
2　怀念肖邦 /176
3　歌 /178
4　万事万物 /180
5　骚动的树木 /182
6　开花的骨头 /184
7　微小的卧室 /186
8　午后的生命 /188
9　多手之躯 /190
10　乱石的岁月 /192
11　潮湿的沉默 /194
12　伸长的躯体 /196
13　夜 /198
14　黑暗的水果 /200
15　鱼 /202
16　月亮的桥 /204
17　已经迟了 /206
18　幽居之歌 /208

## 附录：散文二篇

西湖，或梦想的五个瞬间 /239
数学家与诗人 /249

## 后记

漫游 by蔡天新 /256

# I
# In the ocean of the world
## 世界的海洋

### *我们在世界的海洋上游泳*

1

我们在世界的海洋上游泳
白天的一半没入水中
夜晚的一半浮出水面

2

在阳台上,你看见什么了吗?
春天正驶向另一个码头
这里,那里,不时改变着航向

3

立交桥是坚定的
白色的帆,红色的帆
在一个黄昏撞得粉碎

4

我们在世界的海洋上游泳
死亡是面诱人的旗帜
悬挂在不可企及的桅杆上方

*1991,杭州*

## *In the ocean of the world*

1

We swim in the ocean of the world
our daytime half submerged in the water
our nighttime half floating on the surface

2

From the balcony, what have you seen?
spring sailing to another harbour –
here, there, often changing course

3

The bridge on the overpass is solid
the white sail, the red sail
collide with it and shatter in the dusk

4

We swim in the ocean of the world
death an enticing flag
on top of an unattainable mast

*Hangzhou, 1991*

## 阳 光

太阳是一只芒果
切开就是白天
不切开就是夜晚
我们吞吃阳光
强壮了肌肉
而当我们安寝
阳光汇入了血液
在我们的身体里旅行
它没有停歇
又遇上了另一片阳光

*1989,杭州*

## *Sunlight*

The sun is a mango.
Cut open, it's the day.
Left uncut, the evening.
We swallow sunlight
Making strong muscles.
While we sleep
Sunlight flows into our blood
Travels throughout our body.
On its journey it meets
Another piece of sunlight.

*Hangzhou, 1989*
*trans. James Booze and John Rosenwald*

### 当盛夏沿着蜿蜒的海岸南移

当盛夏沿着蜿蜒的海岸南移
秋天乘虚而入
仿佛水流进入一片空地
我听到了海上传来的歌声
那是昔日恋人卵石般圆润的嗓音
她褪下了裙裾
在一块巨大湿润的礁石上
我倾听着,用一只耳朵
和一颗来自孩提时代的星星

*1992,杭州*

## When summer retreats to the south along the wandering coastline

When summer retreats to the south
along the wandering coastline
fall creeps in, grasping the moment
rushing to saturate parched fields.
I hear a song from the ocean
the sweet voice of an old lover.
Sitting on a reef she takes off her clothes
while I listen attentively with one ear
and one star from my childhood.

*Hangzhou, 1992*
*trans. Michelle Haight and John Rosenwald*

## 散 步

脸向东
鼻子向西

手掌石子般
踢开

指甲割破
大地的血脉

我躺下
潜入河流

倏忽出现
在高山的头顶

*1990，杭州*

## *Stroll*

Face to east
and nose to west

The palm of the hand
kicked out like a roof tile

The nails shear
the blood vessels of the earth

I lie down
dive into the rivers

And appear swiftly
at the head of the mountains

*Hangzhou, 1990*

## *再远一点*

再远一点
我们将看到
人群像砂粒
堆砌在一起
彼此相似

再远一点
我们将看到
房屋像贝壳
或仰或卧
难以分辨

再远一点
我们将看到
城市在陷落
市民们纷纷出逃
搭乘超员的旅客快车

再远一点

*1988,杭州*

## *From higher up*

From higher up
you'll see
crowds like grains of sand
piled together,
all more or less the same.

From higher up
you'll see
houses like seashells
facing up or down
difficult to distinguish.

From higher up
you'll see
a city subsiding
the residents fleeing in droves
in overcrowded express trains.

From higher up

*Hangzhou, 1988*

## 分 割

月光把建筑物的头分割
成三角的形状
圆弧的形状

把悬铃木的枝叶分割
成鸟的形状
羽毛的形状

无垠的大海也被分割
还有我们脆弱的心灵
有谁看见？

*1992，杭州*

## *Division*

The moonlight divides buildingtops
into the shapes of triangles
the shapes of circles and arcs

divides the branches and leaves of plane trees
into the shapes of birds
the shapes of feathers

the boundless sea is also divided
as are our fragile souls –
but who has ever seen them?

*Hangzhou, 1992*

### 关于鱼的诗

我喜欢把汽车看作单词

单词容易改变词性

比如打一个 U 弯

就可以获得形容词

它们相互撞击,在高速公路上

有时会产生全新的句子

把车开进太平洋吧

海水知道如何润色

我们侧身游出车门

顷刻发现一首关于鱼的诗

*1993,加利福尼亚*

## *Poem about fish*

I like to think of cars as words.

It's easy to change the roots of words.

Make a U-turn, for example,

and you will find an adjective.

People bump into each other on the freeway

sometimes creating totally new sentences.

If you drive a car into the Pacific

the sea water will know how to refine it.

When you swim out of the car you will

instantly come across a poem about fish.

*California, 1993*
*trans. James Booze*

### 树木和狗

它们将跟随着你
无论去远方还是邻舍
或遮阳或护膝
把影子投向大地

可是你得学会识辨
它们的年轮和种族
学会像露水和尘土一样
俯向阔叶和卷毛

比起庞大的飞行器来
它们是更为可靠的朋友
甚至当红色的月亮升起
它们也不会消失不见

*2005,奈舍*

## *Trees and dogs*

Trees and dogs will follow you whether you set off
to a distant place or just to the neighbour's
either blocking the sunshine or rubbing against your knees
leaving their shadows on the earth

But you have to learn to recognise
their annual rings and their breeds
and learn, like the dew and the dust
to settle onto big leaves and thick fur

Compared to huge aircraft
they are more reliable friends
even when the red moon rises
they won't disappear

*Nassjo, 2005*

## 湖水

大地是一片湖水
天空是一片湖水
城市是一片湖水
房屋是一片湖水

墙壁是垂立的湖水
椅子是折叠的湖水
茶杯是卷曲的湖水
毛巾是悬挂的湖水

阳光是透明的湖水
音乐是流动的湖水
爱情是感觉的湖水
梦忆是虚幻的湖水

*1994，芝加哥-多伦多*

## *Lake water*

The land is an expanse of lake water
The sky is an expanse of lake water
The city is an expanse of lake water
The house is an expanse of lake water

The wall is vertical lake water
The chair is folded lake water
The teacup is lake water rolled up
The towel is hanging lake water

Sunshine is transparent lake water
Music is flowing lake water
Love is mutual-feeling lake water
The dream is imaginary lake water

*Chicago-Toronto, 1994*

## *如何才能把时间挽留*

如何才能把时间挽留
像一个远方来的亲人
而不是一片落叶随风飘逝

如何才能把时间分割
像青草一样咀嚼、反刍
消化在动物的胃里

如何才能让时间睁大眼睛
加入我们细心的阅读
或随着音乐的节拍起舞

如何才能让时间开口说话
让他站在世界的讲台上
成为我们大众的导师

*1992,杭州*

## *How to ask time to stay*

How to ask time to stay
like family from far off
though not like a leaf driven by wind.

How to cut time
like green grass, ruminating
in the mouth of the beast.

How to wake time to the world
till he reads with our wide eyes
rhythmic, rising to dance.

How to stand time at the lectern
of life, make him make speeches
become our new leader.

*Hangzhou, 1992*
*trans. John Rosenwald*

## 梦想活在世上

树枝从云层中长出
飞鸟向往我的眼睛

乡村和炊烟飘过屋顶
河流挽着我的胳膊出现

月亮如一枚蓝蓝的宝石
嵌入指环

我站到耳朵的悬崖上
梦想活在世上

*1990，杭州*

## *Dream of living in the world*

Branches grow from clouds.
Birds fly eagerly towards my eyes.

Landscape and smoke billow over the house.
Rivers run along my arms.

The moon is a blue sapphire
Set in a ring.

I stand on the precipice of the ear
Dream of living in the world.

*Hangzhou, 1990*
*trans. Michelle Haight and John Rosenwald*

# II
# The small boat of your nose
## 女人之花

**诗**

一个
纯净的
少女

躺在
海边的
沙滩上

她的
头发系
着白云

一起
被浪花
吞没

*1989，杭州*

## *Poem*

  An
innocent
creature

  lying
 on the
sandy shore

her hair
bound by
white clouds

  all
swallowed by
 the sea

*Hangzhou, 1989*
*trans. Michelle Haight*

*女人之花*

她的身躯是一朵花
开放在黑色的凤凰座椅上
她的头颅是花蕊
从皙白的颈项间伸出
这是一朵浮游的花
像大海涌起的雪浪
这朵花在人丛中出现
黄色的花红色的花
修长的大腿如花茎
伸向岌岌可危的大地

*1990,杭州*

## *Flower*

Her body is a flower

blossoming on the saddle of a phoenix bicycle

her head is the pistil

stretching from her clean white neck

a flower that floats

like the white waves of the sea

a flower that appears among people

– a yellow flower, a red flower –

her slender thighs like floral axes

extend into the dangerous earth

*Hangzhou, 1990*

## 裸体

诗歌来到了我的身旁
垂下她长长的手臂
彻夜在我的额上寻找
一片遥远的黑盐之海

那在浪的冠顶上跳跃的鼓点
一个玻璃的夏天的回忆
我失落于我自身之中
两个交织在一起的裸体

*1994，旧金山-蒙特雷*

## *Naked*

Poetry sidles up to me.
All night her long arms
hover over my forehead.
A distant sea of black salt.

Rhythm swims from crest to crest.
A memory from the glass summer.
I draw into myself
like two lovers intertwined.

*San Francisco-Monterey, 1994*
*trans. Michelle Haight and John Rosenwald*

## 心灵的水面

我喜欢在你面前
让你额头的灯光
映照我心灵的水面

那束亮丽的秀发
如村庄散落河岸
芳香随风飘溢

当我俯身向下
你鼻梁的船只
倏然远去

*1991,杭州*

## *The river of my mind*

I like to stand before you
and let the light of your forehead
shine upon the river of my mind

Your luxuriant hair
scatters over the riverbanks like villages
its fragrance floats on the wind

When I move closer
the small boat of your nose
swiftly turns away

*Hangzhou, 1991*

## 长椅

从前我在一张长椅上亲昵过
小红背心后面有一只伸开的手

如今我独自一人坐在地中海滨
眺望着天际下的那一片湛蓝

它是那样的宁静,从不折射阳光
我偶尔扭头去看她披散的长发

她没有吱声,脸孔埋得很深
像一只知了粘贴在高树枝上

*2004,贝鲁特*

## *The bench*

Once I felt intimacy on a long bench
my hand rested on a small red vest

Now I sit alone on the shore of the Mediterranean
looking into the distance, at the deep blue sea

Such tranquillity never reflects the sunlight
Sometimes I turn my head and see her long loose hair

She makes no sound. Her face is buried deeply
like a cicada clinging to a branch.

*Beirut, 2004*

## 绿 风

风来自高楼的峡谷
经过有花瓶的窗台
将一束花的叶子吹落
而让另一束花只留下叶子
风吹在她忧愁的脸上
她的眼睛显得迷惘
风轻轻解开她的衣裙
她的乳房多出一只
风倾压在她身上

*1989，杭州*

## *Green wind*

A breeze winding through the canyon of the buildings

passes over the windowsill with its vase

blowing off all the leaves of one flower

off another all the petals so that only leaves remain

the wind reaches the sad face of a woman

whose eyes show she is lost in thought

the wind gently loosens her clothing

filling her dress with one more breast

the weight of the wind lies full length along her body

*Hangzhou, 1989*

## 芙蓉湖

一次我驾舟在芙蓉湖上
一位少女在岸边沉入遐思
她夏装的扣眼里闪烁着微光
我驶近她,向她发出邀请

她惊讶,继而露出了笑容
暮色来到我们中间,缩短了
万物的距离,一颗隐微的痣
比书籍亲近,比星辰遥远

*1992,厦门-杭州*

## *Lotus Lake*

Once while rowing on Lotus Lake, I saw
a young woman deep in thought on the shore
the buttons glinting on her summer dress.
Rowing closer, I invited her to join me.

At first I startled her, but then she smiled.
Twilight fell around us, shortening
all distances ; a subtle beauty spot
closer than a book, further than a star

*Xiamen, 1992*
*trans. James Booze*

## 数字与玫瑰

毕达哥拉斯在直角三角形的斜边上
弹拨乐曲,一边苦苦地构想着
那座水晶般透明的有理数迷宫
他的故乡在爱琴海的萨摩斯岛
从小就没有想要做水手,也没有被
萨洛尼卡城里的漂亮姑娘诱惑
数字成为他心中最珍重的玫瑰
那些绯红、橙黄或洁白的花朵
巧妙地装饰着无与伦比的头脑
敦促其写下著名的断言:万物皆数
佛罗伦萨的莱昂拉多曾设法凑近
把妩媚的小美人吉勒芙拉撂在一旁
终于因为体格的缘故半途而废

*2000,麦德林*

## *The number and the rose*

Pythagoras played music on the hypotenuse

while devising the system of rational numbers
a labyrinth as transparent as quartz
his home was on Samos on the Aegean Sea
as a child he never wanted to be a sailor
nor was he ever enticed by the beautiful girls of Salonika
numbers were the treasured roses of his heart
those crimson, orange, yellow, or pure white flowers
were the perfect expressions of his unequalled mind
urging him to write his famous assertion "all things are numbers"
Leonardo once, in Florence, devoted himself to this principle
neglecting the charms of the young beauty Genevra
finally giving up for reasons we don't know

*Medellin, 2000*

## 笛卡尔

岛屿存在了数千年
一个衰落的贵族之家
像伊比利亚的维加

海平面悄悄地上升
几何体隐匿在水下
不安、敏感、生性孤僻

等待船只和旗帜
等待克里斯蒂娜女王
徒然把灵魂的激情奉献

*1994,加利福尼亚*

## *Descartes*

Like the De Vegas of Spain
like an island thousands of years old
he was born into a noble family in decline

Just as the sea level rises quietly
and its lonely geometry hides under water
he was restless, sensitive, eccentric

He waited for the ship to collect him
sent by Queen Christiana
so he could offer his fervent soul in vain

*California, 1994*

## *夜 航*

1

她端坐不动
双臂怀抱
谜一样诱人的
等腰四边形

2

当她抬起头
那棕色发架下
两颗鲜嫩的葡萄
迅速被我吞吃

3

美腿舒展
仿佛停滞的钟摆
海浪在增高
睡意在减少

4

嫣然一笑
露出两行牙齿
犹如开裂的石榴
悬浮在空气中

*1999,爱琴海*

## *Overnight boat*

### 1

She sits quite still
arms folded into an
isosceles quadrilateral
fascinating as a riddle

### 2

When she lifts her head
her eyes under her brown hair
are like two fresh and tender grapes
which I devour greedily

### 3

Her beautiful leg stretches
like a motionless pendulum
the sea's waves swell
and my sleep evaporates

### 4

She smiles fleetingly
revealing two lines of teeth
like a pomegranate
suspended open in the air

*Aegean Sea, 1999*

## 回声

如果你以为
如果你以为
这座房子
倒塌以后
倒塌以后
我们的故事
就会就会
结束结束
你和我你和我
会重新重新
开始生活
你　错　啦
　　　错　啦

*1990，杭州*

## *Echo*

If you think
if you think
once this house
falls down
falls down
our story
will now will now
be over be over
you and I you and I
like new like new
will start to live
you   are   wrong
      you   are   wrong

*Hangzhou, 1990*
*trans. John Rosenwald*

# III
# The highest pleasure

最高乐趣

## *漫游*

我在五色的人海里漫游
林间溪流中飘零的一片草叶

一切都是水,一切都是水
时间自身的船体掉过头来

顺着它蜿蜒的航线而下
一座白柱子的宅第耸立在河岸

斑鸠的飞翔划破了天空的宁静
远处已是一片泛紫色的群山

*1993,加利福尼亚*

## *Wandering*

I wander the colourful sea of human beings
like a leaf drifting in a forest stream

Everything is in the water, everything is in the water
Time itself is turned round like the prow of a ship

floating along a winding route
a house with white pillars stands on the river bank

a soaring wild dove cuts through the sky's tranquillity
in the distance the hills are a saturated purple

*California, 1993*

## 罗马古道

从前我曾走过这条路
风景依然历历在目
隧道、小溪、葡萄园

铁道线弯来又弯去
同样是上上下下的乘客
只不过会说英语的人多了

亚平宁的雨斜落在玻璃上
时光犹如暮色中的炊烟
飘走了又被风吹回来

但那只是偶然的相聚
如果你遇见旧时的恋人
最好把她当成一次回忆

*2005，罗马-佛罗伦萨*

## *Ancient road*

I've travelled this road once before
the scenery still comes clearly into view –
the tunnel, the stream and the vineyard.

The railway line has many turns
passengers get on or off as before
only these days more of them speak English.

The Appennine rain falls slanting on the windows
and time like chimney smoke floats away
only to be blown back by the wind.

Everything happens only once –
if you meet an old lover
best regard her as a recollection.

*Rome-Florence, 2005*

## 尼亚加拉瀑布

蓝色之上的白色
被蓝色包围的白色
像沉溺于梦幻的死亡

鸟的羽毛多于游人的发丝
鸟的嘴唇比情侣的嘴唇
更早触及云母的雨帘

我随意说出几个名字
让它们从水上漂走
和黑夜一起降临

一枚失血的太阳颤抖了
向死亡再进一步
一千只冰凉的手伸入我的后颈项

*1994,纽约-安大略*

## *Niagara Falls*

Above the blue, white.
Surrounded by blue, white,
like death wallowing in illusions.

Birds with more feathers than tourists' hair.
Earlier than lovers' lips, the birds lips
kiss the curtain of rain.

Relaxed, I release
names into the water. They float off
as night falls.

A pale sun shivers. One step
closer to death. Thousands of icy hands
brush the nape of my neck.

*New York-Ontario, 1994*
*translated by John Rosenwald*

### 夏奈的海浪

没有沙漏
我用睫毛的闪动
和乌鸦的羽毛
计时

天空曾经湛蓝
如今却被水仙
和大象的鼻子
挤占

我们下着跳棋
正当湿婆在
在一座寺庙里
端坐

孟加拉湾起风了
一撮黝黑的头发
被夏奈的海浪
卷起

*2003，班加罗尔*

## *The waves of Chennai*

Without an hourglass
I use the blink of my eyelash
and the feathers of a crow
to tell the time

The sky once deep blue
is now occupied
by narcissus flowers
and the trunks of elephants

We play chinese checkers
while Shiva
sits upright
inside the temple

A breeze over the Bay of Bengal
a lock of dark hair
is lifted by
the waves of Chennai

*Bangalore, 2003*

## 棕榈

躯干高大、挺拔
用来营造房屋
绿色的枝桠和长叶
用来搭建篷顶

果实的颜色
由浅灰变殷红
再转紫或黑
用来喂母猪和公牛

小小的草丛
用来储存雨水
粗壮的手臂,支撑起
一个穷苦的国家

*2000,哈瓦那*

## *Palm trees*

Trunks tall and straight
for building houses
Branches and long leaves
for making roofs

The colour of the fruit
changes from grey to dark red
then to purple or black
to feed pigs and cattle

Halfway up a grass armpit
traps and stores rain water
The sturdy arms support
a poverty-stricken country

*La Habana, 2000*

## 爆炸

空气推开了空气
柔软的事物积蓄了更多的力量
敏感、细致,毫不犹豫
人们在瞬间抵达了天堂

而我从忧烦的睡梦中惊醒
打开那扇通往屋顶平台的铁门
发现又一个春光明媚的早晨
已如空气一样潜伏下来

*2000,麦德林*

## *Explosion*

The air shoved the air forward
soft with accumulated power
sensitive careful unhesitating
people arrived in heaven instantly

I awake from a sad and worried sleep
open the steel gate to the roof of the building
find a beautiful spring morning
already lying in wait like the air

*Medellin, 2000*

## 厄尔布尔士山

它高高在上
把外高加索的寒风阻拦
也把里海的鱼阻拦

斯文·赫定曾经策马扬鞭
从它的夹缝中穿行而过
带着诺迪克人的稚气

像一枚古旧的邮票
贴在天空的信笺上
被旅行者用剪刀裁下

*2004,德黑兰*

## *The Erburz mountains*

Soaring high up
they stop the cold from Transcaucasia
and the fish of the Caspian Sea

Once Sven Hedin cracking his whip
rode through their crevices
in his Nordic naivety

Stuck like an ancient stamp
on the letter of the sky
to be cut out by the traveller's scissors

*Teheran, 2004*

## 细流

在伊斯法罕旅店的庭院里
喷泉的细流潺潺不息
一整个夜晚陪伴在枕边

两个波斯少女住在隔壁
她们有时说话,有时消失
像高原上的河流

一株硕大的椰枣树耸立在窗外
在没有月光的夜晚它就是月光
静静地照耀着细流和梦

*2004,伊斯法罕*

## *Trickle*

In the garden of an inn at Esfahan
a trickle murmuring from a fountain
shares my pillow the whole night

The voices of two Persian girls
speak and vanish in the next room
like rivers on the Plateau of Iran

A gigantic date palm stands outside the window
it is the moonlight in a night without moonlight
shining calmly on the fountain and the dream

*Esfahan, 2004*

## 朗 诵

铜锤敲响并不意味着丰收季节的来临
那穿短袖衬衫的钢琴师挥舞着双臂
在听众的感官全部打开之后
女主持用一种委婉的语调说话

可我们住在彩虹桥的另一头
把洗净的衣服晾在银河树的枝桠上
或许我们对地球已无话可说
各自驾着布兰登堡门顶上的马车离去

*2004，柏林*

## *The reading*

A gong is struck but not for the harvest season
a pianist in a shortsleeved shirt brandishes his arms
after they get the audience's full attention
the hostess speaks in a measured tone

But we live at the other end of the rainbow
dry our clothes on the trees of the Milky Way
Perhaps we have no words to say to the Earth
we ride away on the horses of the Brandenburg gate

*Berlin, 2004*

## 飞行

当飞机盘旋,上升
抵达预想的高度
就不再上升

树木和飞鸟消散
浮云悄悄地翻过了
厚厚的脊背

临窗俯瞰,才发现
河流像一支藤蔓
纠缠着山脉

一座奢华的宫殿
在远方出现
犹如黄昏的一场游戏

所有的往事、梦想和
人物,包括书籍
均已合掌休息

*2000,麦德林*

## *Flight*

The airplane circles up
to cruising altitude
to rise no higher.

Trees and birds disappear
floating clouds quietly
turn over.

Look out the window
you'll see the river like a creeper
clinging to the sierra.

A luxurious palace
appears in the distance
like a children's game at dusk.

All past things –
dreams, people and books
rest with their palms closed.

*Medellin, 2000*

### 最高乐趣

请客人们旅行吧
美丽的金斑蛾
鼹鼠绯红的手

开蜡花的灌木丛
小溪的喧响之流
青草在身后起伏不定

人们在树上涂抹糖浆
罗得之妻在逃离时回望
顷刻化为一根盐柱

夜晚不知道夜晚的吟唱
孤独不知道孤独的美妙
没有时间的最高乐趣

*1993,加利福尼亚*

## *The highest pleasure*

Let them travel, the guests –
the beautiful moth with gold spots
the mole with bright red hands

the shrubbery blooming with morning glories
the stream with its bubbling sound
and the green grass rippling behind

Somebody paints syrup on a tree
Lot's wife looks back and suddenly
changes into a pillar of salt

Night does not know the night's own melody
loneliness does not know the marvel of loneliness
the highest pleasure is outside of time

*California, 1993*

# IV
# Green blood

绿血

## 绿 血

我从北方回来,夜已经很深
我进屋后返身关门
发现了台阶下的树叶
这是从被台风刮倒的
法国梧桐上掉下的
树的躯干已被拖走
我好像看见一摊血
淤积在石板地上
我记得双亲大人喜欢
在树下乘凉,稍歇
谈论他们的孙子
我甚至记得他们
费劲吐出褐色瓜子的情景
那是在去年夏天
今年夏天,我不知道
今年夏天他们将怎样度过

*1988,杭州*

## *Green blood*

Coming back from the north in deep night
I enter my home, turn, closing the door
find on the steps sycamore leaves
left by the typhoon
limbs and trunk already dragged off.
I thought I saw pools of blood
coagulated on the ground.
I remember my parents kept cool
under this tree as they talked
of their grandson, remember
the scene, even remember them
spitting black seeds as they sat.
That was last summer.
This summer, I do not know,
this summer, how they will spend their time.

*Hangzhou, 1988*
*trans. John Rosenwald*

# 湖

### 1

明亮清澈的水面
燕子在天空飞翔

对于小小的湖泊
它就是一架歼击机

### 2

两支木桨摇响
一个瘦瘦的老家伙

滋润的船体
委身于湖面

### 3

青山倒映在湖中
那碧绿的水波下

可有烈炎的森林
鱼儿和猎人一起巡游

## *Lake*

### 1

Over the bright clear surface
a swallow flies through the sky

to this tiny lake
it is a fighter plane

### 2

Two wooden paddles swung
by a thin old man

the wet hull
cleaves to the surface

### 3

The lake mirrors the mountains
below the deep green wave

perhaps there's a tropical forest there
where fish and hunters patrol

4

一阵微弱的凉风吹过
湖上漾起了层层涟漪

湖水的心事重重
徒有冷漠的外表

5

一大群人爬上了岸
他们的面孔像鱼鳞

阳光似刀片切割下来
被茂密的树枝遮拦

6

黑夜来到我们的周围
有人扔下一块石子

可以听见一种声音
在湖上久久地回荡

*1996,杭州*

4

A faint cool breeze
ripples over the lake

the lake has many worries
it only appears to be indifferent

5

People swarm from the water to the shore
their faces like scales of fish

sunlight cuts like a blade
blocked by thick branches

6

Darkness shrouds us
someone throws in a stone

its sound persists
reverberating

*Hangzhou, 1996*

## 宝石山

柳丝漂漾在湖上
被一簇簇桃花
分隔

断桥向西
雨点一样密集的情侣
向西

早春二月
青郁的宝石山上
是谁的嘴唇开口说话

*1994,弗雷斯诺*

## *Baoshi Hill*

The leaves of willows ripple above West Lake
alternating one peach, one willow
with the peach trees in blossom

Towards the west of Broken Bridge
lovers crowd like raindrops
towards the west

It is February, early spring
on the abundant green of Baoshi Hill
whose lips open and speak?

*Fresno, 1994*

## 故乡的美人

多年以后我返回了故乡，
在一口古老废弃的水井边
遇到了从前镇上的美人。
她少女一般轻盈的体态，以及

从舌尖发出的哧哧的笑声
既让我惊讶又感到亲切。我想起
那些游历过的地方，想起
那些妇女，她们相异的舞姿

犹如波浪把时光分隔，把我们
分隔。恍忽之间，她已经
车身离去，只留下一个背影
又教我想起她年轻时的丰韵。

*2000，麦德林*

## *The beauty from my hometown*

Many years later I return to my childhood home
and run into the former beauty of the town
near the abandoned ancient well.
Her carriage is lithe as a young girl's, and

her laughter ripples from the tip of her tongue.
Surprised by her, I feel tenderness. It reminds me
of all the places I have travelled,  all
the women I have seen, the way they dance

just like the waves which divide time and divide us.
While I was lost in thought, she'd already turned
and walked away, leaving just her departing form
reminding me of her charm when she was young.

*Medellin, 2000*

## 回想之翼

当我忆及遥远的往昔
怀着兴味,听从幻想的劝告
一双因患冻疮而肿大的手
在白色的窗帘布后出现
一位死去很久的亲人的脸
一片淡紫色的幽远
被一个感觉的鼹鼠丘破坏
像一座石板地的旧式楼房
以此伤害了黑夜的眼睑
一把精心制作的扶手椅
和一个并不丰富的藏书架
回想之翼的两次扑动

*1994,弗雷斯诺*

## *Wings of recollection*

When urged by curiosity, obeying fantasy
I recall my remote past –
a pair of hands swollen with frostbite
appear behind a white curtain
the face of someone close who died long ago
a distant lavender-coloured memory
which changes into a mousehole
and then into an old-style house with a flagstone floor
which injures the eyelid of dark night
then changes again into an armchair carefully made
and a bookshelf with a few books
two flaps of the wings of recollection

*Fresno, 1993*

## 橡 皮

萤火虫闪烁着从窗外飞过
青蛙在田野里有节奏地鸣叫
屋子里女人的交谈继续着
男孩坐在我身边,悄悄地

把手伸进花布短裤的内侧
快感像波浪,迅速流遍全身
随后是新一轮的迷藏,直到
母亲们厌倦了古老的话题

我躺着,回味适才那个梦
盯住那双行将缩回的手
仿佛过去年代的一丁点亮光
延伸到万里之外的今夜

*2000,麦德林*

## *Hide and seek*

Outside the window, fireflies flash.
In the field, the rhythm of croaking frogs.
In the room, our mothers talk heart-to-heart.
The boy next to me quietly searching for the eraser

tucks a hand into my khaki shorts.
Pleasure, like waves, washes swiftly over my body.
Then a new round, my turn,
till our mothers tire of the old topics.

I lie now, reminiscing,
eyes focused on that hand withdrawing
like a flash of light, stretching
from then to now, thousands of miles away.

*Medellin, 2000*
*trans. John Rosenwald and Robert Berold*

## 村姑在有篷盖的拖拉机里远去

我在乡村大路上行走
一辆拖拉机从身后驶过
我悠然回眸的瞬间
和村姑的目光遽然相遇

在迅即逝去的轰鸣声中
矩形的篷盖蓦然变大
它将路边的麦田挤缩到
我无限扩张的视域一隅

而她头上的围巾飘扬如一面旗帜
她那硕大无朋的脚丫
从霍安·米罗的画笔下不断生长
一直到我伸手可触

*1988年，杭州*

## *Country girl receding on a covered tractor*

While I was walking on a village road
a tractor came up from behind
and the very moment I turned my head
I looked into the eyes of a country girl

As soon as the rumbling noise had passed
the awning of the trailor grew instantly huge
making the wheatfield beside the road shrink
to a small corner of my infinite sight

But the scarf on her head still flutters like a flag
and her feet are larger than life
as if they'd grown from the brush of Joan Miro
continually stretching towards my outstretched hand

*Hangzhou, 1988*

## 疑 问

把头伸出有铁栏的窗户外
把椅子敲碎在膝盖面前
冬天的风从梧桐的肚皮上溜走
落叶的影子在泥土上摇曳并消失
犹如雪飘在湖上被水溶化
大人物坐着轿车去上班
孩子们被一个个小小的愿望驱赶
我们活在这个世界上
像一梭子弹穿过暗夜的墙

*1989,杭州*

## *Query*

Squeezes through the window's burglar bars
Breaks a chair into pieces over his knee
The winter wind sneaks away from the belly of the plane trees
The shadow of fallen leaves drags on the ground and vanishes
Like snow which falls into a lake and dissolves into the water
Important people commute to their offices in chaffeur-driven cars
While children are propelled around by one small desire
We live in this world like a volley of bullets
passing through the wall of the dark night

*Hangzhou, 1989*

## *保留的记忆*

我记得那是一个夏天
一只绿色的甲壳虫
在我摊开的诗集上爬行
它来到大卫·依格纳托的名字旁
久久不肯离去
它参与了我的阅读
我满怀喜悦的心情
用最小的手指
轻轻摁着它的腹部
转眼之间
它已经躺在那儿
变成了一行注记
它分享了我的快乐
一直保留在我的记忆里

*1988，杭州*

## *The persistence of memory*

I remember it was summer:
a green beetle, crawling
on my open volume of poems
paused alongside the name David Ignatow.
For a long time not wanting to leave
it joined my reading. Joyfully,
using my littlest finger,
I delicately touched its belly.
In the flick of an eye
it already lay there
turned to a footnote.
It shared my happiness
forever persists in my memory.

*Hangzhou, 1988*
*trans. John Rosenwald*

## 跳 绳

每一棵光洁的稻草
都布满了银色的月光
它们被编织成绳索

就像脚踝上的链子
那圆圈中的圆圈
也布满了银色的月光

无论眉梢、鬓角
还是手臂上的烫痕
反来复去地穿梭往来

*2005，马尼拉*

## *Skipping*

Each bright and clean rice stalk
is covered entirely in silver moonlight
and then woven into the rope.

Like a silver chain on the ankle
the circle around the circle
also covered in moonlight

The tip of the eyebrow, the temple
and the scald mark on the arm
all oscillate through the rope.

*Manila, 2005*

## 在水边

黄昏来临，犹如十万只寒鸦，
在湖上翻飞；而气温下降，
到附近的山头，像西沉的落日
消失在灌木丛中。

我独自低吟浅唱，在水边，
用舌头轻拍水面，溅击浪花。
直到星星出现，在歌词中，
潸然泪下。

*1991，杭州*

## *At the water's edge*

Dusk approaches.  Thousands of cold crows
gather above the lake.  The temperature drops
to the top of a nearby hill,  the sunset in the west
vanishing in the shrubbery.

At the water's edge, I sing in a low voice,
imagine lapping the water with my tongue
until stars appear, and the words of the song,
and the lines of tears.

*Hangzhou, 1991*

# V
# Americas

美洲

### 的的喀喀湖

在利马候机时
天空已乌云密布

库斯科在左侧
仅在航路图上显现

看不见蓝色的天空
只见到深蓝的湖水

假如真的有愚公
搬走那些岩石和泥土

湖水会悬于空中
威力胜过南极的冰川

4/2016，利马-拉巴斯

## *Lake Titicaca*

When we were at Lima airport
The sky was covered with dark clouds

Now we're in the air
The flight map shows Cuzco on the left

We can't see the blue sky
But only the dark blue lake

If old man Yu was here
Who could move rocks and soil

The water of the lake would hang in the air
As powerful as an Antarctic glacier

*Lima - La Paz, April 2016,*

*拉巴斯*

黄色的建筑物直通山顶
顺坡而下,有些平行的街道
愈往低处愈加开阔和拥堵

总统府和部长楼也建在谷底
每天早上五点灯光会亮起
那有助于体察和安抚民心

游客们有的咀嚼古柯叶
不会嚼的就用叶子泡茶
以便抵御高原缺氧的病症

奶酪和木薯搅拌在一起
在烤箱里分泌出一种醇香
色泽犹似包裹粽子的玉米叶

而东南方向的伊利玛尼峰
高高在上,像一只白头翁
俯瞰并守护着拉巴斯城

*4/2016,拉巴斯-科帕卡巴拉*

## *La Paz*

Yellow buildings march to the top of the hill
On the slope, the streets run parallel
Further down they're more congested

The presidential palace is in the valley below
Its lights come on at five each morning
which reassures the people

Some of the visitors chew coca leaves
Others use the leaves to make tea
It keeps the high altitude sickness away

The host bakes cheese and cassava cakes
Their colour the corn leaves that wrap dumplings
The oven gives off a lovely smell

Mount Illimani in southeast
High above, like a bald eagle
Watches over the city of La Paz

*La Paz - Copacabala, April 2016,*

## 库斯科

许多人是为了去马丘比丘
迫不得已才经过库斯科
甚至第一次听说了她

其实在古代很长时间里
这是一个庞大帝国的都城
统治着今天邻近的国家

她趁机展示自己的美丽
尤其那几座广场及其周边
拱形的建筑和长形的瓦片

到了夜里,阳台传出了笑声
阳台上面的灯饰像是柳眉
一轮圆月从芦苇上方升起

4/2016,库斯科-达拉斯

## *Cuzco*

Many people pass through Cuzco
It's on the route to Machu Picchu
Some are seeing it for the first time.

But in ancient times
It was the capital of a great empire
which later broke up into several countries

The city shows off its unique beauty
in its squares, stone arches
and elongated roof tiles

At night there is laughter from the balcony
The lamp above is like an eyebrow
A full moon rises over the reeds

*Cuzco-Dallas, April 2016*

## 长 城

当我飞越落基山脉
看见了一座白色的长城
在山峦顶上迂回曲折

后来我与科罗拉多河相伴
又见到一座地下的长城
深不见底,激流勇退

*4/2016,达拉斯-旧金山*

## *The Great Wall*

As I flew over the Rocky Mountains
The mountain range was a Great Wall
White with many twists and turns


Later beside the Colorado River
I found another Great Wall underground
Bottomless and old-man angry


*Dallas - San Francisco, April 2016*

## 金门大桥

从看见一艘巨轮
到它消失在天际
只是一眨眼的功夫

从一个月亮
到半个月亮
也只是一眨眼的功夫

从二十三年前初见
到此番重游
依然是一眨眼的功夫

*4/2016，旧金山*

## *Golden Gate Bridge*

The moment of watching a huge ship
Till it disappears on the horizon
Is just a blink of an eye

The time lapse from full moon
To half moon
Is also a blink of an eye

My first sight of this bridge
was 23 years ago
still only a blink of an eye

*San Francisco, April 2016*

## 去往圣芭芭拉途中

### ——给张益唐

五号公路洛杉矶转十号
向西到桑塔莫妮卡
尔后沿一号公路北上

黄色的野花与大海相伴
海葵在浅水坑里闪耀
退潮以后,身姿更为舒展

海狮在木桥下面独坐
仍然想着莫名的重重心事
忽而又潜入了太平洋

鸥鸟在细软的沙滩上行走
与礁石保持等距离
恰如一对相邻的素数

*4/2016,洛杉矶尔湾*

## *On the way to Santa Barbara*

*for Zhang Yitang*

Take Freeway No. 5, transfer to No 10
At LA, turn west to Santa Monica
then follow Freeway 1 to the north

You'll find yellow wildflowers besides the ocean
and sea anemones bright in shallow water
At low tide, they seem to relax

A sea lion sits alone
under a wooden bridge, preoccupied --
then dives suddenly into the Pacific

While the seagulls walking on the soft sand
keep a constant distance from the rocks
like a pair of twin prime numbers

*Irvine - Los Angeles, April 2016*

### *博厄里俱乐部*

七位诗人来自三个国度
依次走上了博厄里
小小的舞台中央

其中一位男士来自
澳大利亚昆士兰州
洪水适才淹没了他的故乡

一身黑衣头戴黑礼帽
他开始慢条斯理地朗诵
幕间休息时套上一条红裙

他抱了抱美丽的女主持
又热吻一位风度翩翩的听众
事先征得他女伴的同意

最后我们一起走上舞台
谢幕,数十位听众同时起立
鼓掌,为曼哈顿的这个夜晚

*02/2011,纽约-休斯顿*

## *Bowery Poetry Club*

Seven poets from three countries
Climbed up onto the small stage

One came from
Queensland province, Australia
A flood had just drowned his hometown

He wore a black shirt and a black hat
and began to read in a leisurely manner
then at the interval put on a red skirt

He embraced the beautiful hostess
then kissed a graceful man in the audience
(first asking his girlfriend's permission)

At the end we stood together onstage
bowed to the encore: the audience applauding
our night in Manhattan

*New York - Houston, February 2011*

## 波士顿

B是三座桥梁连接两岸
被一个清澈的海湾填充

O是海洋,潮涨时分
带来的是贝壳和青春

S是天空,几乎一片纯蓝
惟有一撮云,携来远方尘埃

T是我造访她的次数
不多不少,刚好三回

O还是海洋,潮退时分
遗落的是珍珠和知识

N是我的名字,两记尾声
拒绝是人类本能的需要

*6/2011,波士顿-普罗维登斯*

## *Boston*

B is the three bridges connecting both sides
surrounded by a clear bay

O is the ocean, when the tide rises
bringing with it sea-shells and young people

S is the sky, almost pure blue
With only a tiny cloud bringing dust from far away

The number of times I visited here
no more or less than that, just three

O is the ocean again, at low tide
draining always pearls and knowledge

N is where my name ends and where No begins
and refusal is an instinctive human need

*Providence - Boston, June 2011*

## 哈佛广场

这座三角形状的广场
疑似哈佛的精神所在
牵狗的嬉皮士出入其中
有的夹着彩色的尾巴

布拉特尔剧场的戏台
拉布迪克的巧克力屋
都不及这里的景致迷人

地铁红线绵延至此
从台阶上走出或进入
人们带走了坎布里奇
最初或最后的记忆

游人依然如潮水涌来
从那排敞开的拱门口消失
可以看看世界的末日和来世

*06/2011，波士顿-普罗维登斯*

## *Harvard Square*

This square has a triangular shape
Which I guess shows Harvard's spirit of fun
The hippies come and go with their dogs
Both they and the dogs have colourful tails

Neither the stage of the Blatter Theatre

Nor La Budke's chocolate house
Are as charming as this scenery

The red line subway reaches here
People step on or off the platform
Taking with them their first or latest
Memories of Cambridge

Visitors arrive like waves of the sea
Then disappear through the row of arches
Where they can watch the end of the world

*Providence - Boston, June 2011*

## 魁北克

纽芬兰省在它的东边
接纳了英格兰的移民

拉布拉多半岛也在东边
阻拦了格陵兰漂来的冰山

需要飞行两个半小时
才能到达哈德逊海峡

险些成为独立的国家
错过了妙龄的贞德公主

*06/2011,魁北克-纽约*

## *Quebec*

Newfoundland province is on the east coast
It was settled by immigrants from England

The Labrador Peninsula, also in the east
stops the icebergs drifting over from Greenland

One has to fly for two and half hours
In order to reach the Hudson Strait

Quebec almost became an independent country
It would not have known about Joan of Arc

*Quebec - New York, June 2011*

## 温哥华

在我早年的一次旅途中
听说过温哥华上尉的故事
浓雾锁住了海峡和春天
无人穿越那黄昏的静谧

一场大雨浇灭了篝火
也令水手把思乡之情收起
在古老暖流的授意之下
他们把家安置在岸边

而当我飞越浩瀚的太平洋
再一次来到这片土地上
想象故友的容貌和笑意
看到灯火如指尖一样亮起

*09/2006，多伦多-蒙特利尔*

## *Vancouver*

On a journey many years ago
I heard the story of Captain Vancouver:
Thick fog blocked the passage through the strait
No one could cross the quietness of dusk

Then a heavy rain drowned out the campfire
And the sailors forgot their longing for home
Encouraged by the ancient warm current
They made their homes on the shore

I flew across the vast ocean
And returned once more to this land
Imagining the face and smile of an old friend
The lights there shining like fingertips

*Montreal - Toronto, September 2006*

# VI
# Far and near
# 远和近

## 远 方

总是被远方吸引
总是被移动的风景吸引
只有当鸟儿回旋在稻田之上
才注意到那一片金黄
只有当风儿吹过
摇响身边的那棵桃树
才发现它的枝丫影子绰约
只有当阳光猛烈地照射到脸上
才发现葡萄园的绿色浓于青草
远方的色泽暗淡下来
但它仍然十分迷人

*2007，拉芬尼*

## *Distant places*

I'm always attracted by distant places,

Always attracted by floating scenery –

Only when the bird circles the rice-field,

Do i notice its golden colour.

Only when the wind blows over

And rattles the peach-tree by my side,

Do i find the shadow of its branches graceful.

Only when the sun shines fiercely on my face,

Do i find that the vineyard greener than the grass,

In the distance colours are veiled

But all the more enchanting.

*Lavigny, 2007*

## 南印度花园

松鼠的尾巴闪过窗台
一片羽毛飘零在空中
棕榈树下昆虫的鸣叫
淹没了附近市井的喧闹

蓝孔雀带回北方的消息
沐浴的人们浸泡在恒河里
不停地洗涤私念和欲望
大象的鼻子层层卷曲

我从未如此亲近地
与动物们生活在一起
比天空中那些漫漫的长夜
更能观照自己的内心

*2003,班加罗尔*

## *South Indian Garden*

A squirrel-tail brushes the window-sill.
A plume falls from the sky.
Insects sing under the palm trees
drowning the noise of the market nearby.

A blue peacock brings news from the North.
People bathe in the Ganges
washing away selfish motives and desires,
while the trunks of the elephants curl.

I have never been so close
to animals, living together —
I can see my heart more clearly now
than during those long night-flights.

*Bangalore, 2003*
*trans. Sudeep Sen*

## 八度海峡

在美丽的喀拉拉海岸
有一座古老的港市卡利卡特
郑和的船队曾在那里停歇
他的遗骨至今下落不明

当他穿过凶险的八度海峡
向南,去往马尔代夫
与梦想着拥有黄金和香料的
葡萄牙人不期而遇

在那个到处布满礁石的地方
他听见渡鸦的鸣叫,继续向西
沿着阿拉伯海和印度洋的
分界线,驶向摩加迪沙

*2003,班加罗尔*

## *Octave Strait*

On the beautiful shores of Kerala
lies the old port town of Calicut.
The fleet of Zheng He once docked here.
His bones lie buried here, still unknown.

As he passed through the Octave Strait
enroute southwards to the Maldives,
he met by chance the Portuguese
with their dreams of spices and gold.

Over the sea strewn with rocks
He heard the cries of ravens
between the Arabian Sea and the Indian Ocean,
as he sailed slowly to Mogadishu.

*Bangalore, 2003*
*trans. Sudeep Sen*

## 从莫斯科到圣彼得堡

看得见的是森林
看不见的也是森林

夜晚的尽头是白昼
白昼的尽头也是白昼

太阳出现又消失了
月亮消失又出现了

火车一路未曾停歇
多少熟悉的面孔浮现

*2016,俄罗斯*

## *From Moscow to St Petersburg*

What we can see is the forest
What we cannot see is also the forest

At the end of night is the day
At the end of day is also the day

The sun appears then disappears
The moon disappears then appears

Never once in the journey did the train stop
And so many famous faces arose in my mind

*Russia, 2016*

## 日内瓦湖

那浅蓝之中的一片深蓝
仿佛岛屿侧卧在大海中
纹丝不动,惟有阳光
才能改变它们的比例和大小

高高在上的阿尔卑斯山
赋予它清凉刺骨的源泉
惟有我潦草的诗行和字句
悠游其中,吸纳四周的景色

*2007,拉芬尼*

## *Lake Geneva*

Deep blue in light blue
an island lies on its side.
Absolutely still, with only sunshine
changing its shape and size.

High up in the distance the Alps
provide cool springs which freeze
my rough verse so that only words
can swim in it, and absorb the view.

*Lavigny, 2007*

## 三河城

一座细巧的城市
傍依着一条宽广的河流

如同一只幼小的蜜蜂
停留在一只硕大的向日葵上

河流流向
无边无际的大海

向日葵围绕着
生生不息的太阳

*2008,三河城-蒙特利尔*

## *Trois-Rivières*

A small delicate city
beside a wide river

Like a tiny bee
nestled in a huge sunflower

The river flows into
the boundless ocean

The sunflower turns round
the neverending sun

*Trois-Rivières - Montreal, 2008*

## 远和近

湖水离开我太远了
无论激荡还是恬静
都无法看清它的波浪

正如体内的那支河流
因为离开我太近了
难以分辨它的方向和源头

*2007，拉芬尼*

## *Far and near*

the lake water is too far from me.
whether it is troubled or peaceful,
i cannot see its waves clearly.

like the river within my body,
it is too close to me —
i cannot tell its direction or source.

*Lavigny, 2007*

## *睡眠与写作*

在漫长的旅途中
除了吃喝拉撒
尚有两件事情可做

不要看科幻电影
不要翻阅航空杂志
甚至不要插上耳机

也不要与邻座交谈
在睡眠的间歇写作
在写作的间歇睡觉

在漫长的旅途中
往事如云一般涌来
又像雾那样溜走

2016，达拉斯-旧金山

## *Sleeping and writing*

On a long journey
Apart from eating drinking and peeing
There are two other things to do

Don't watch science fiction movies
Don't read the inflight magazines
Don't even put on your headphones

Don't talk to the person next to you
Just write and sleep
Sleep and write

On a long journey
Memories arrive like clouds
And slip away like fog

*Dallas-San Francisco, 2016*

### *青海湖*

如果这湖底有一个洞
那它另一头必定通向
地中海的蔚蓝海岸
雪莱在一场风暴中死去

我们在湖边吟诵
没有等到冬天来临
便已逐一离去
也没有看见春天的沙尘

在青藏高原的边沿
她安闲地卧躺着
恰似一只小绵羊
委身于一片青草地

*2011，西宁-杭州*

## Qinghai Lake

If there was a hole in the bottom of the lake
The other end would appear in
The sky-blue coast of the Mediterranean
Where Shelley perished in a sudden storm

On the lake shore, we recite poetry
It is before the beginning of winter
We left, one by one,
Before seeing the sandstorms of spring

On the edge of the Tibetan plateau
She lies in peaceful repose
Like a baby lamb throwing herself
Into a green meadow

*Xining-Hangzhou, 2011*

## 冬天到来的时候

冬天到来的时候
会有一场暴风雪
在宝石山上空聚集
雪花会飘落我的阳台
会覆盖毕毕的爪印

冬天到来的时候
在小兴安岭的某个村庄
会有少年爬上一列货车
去到很远很远的城市
寻找医生救治他的父亲

*10/2013，利马-上海*

## *When winter comes*

When winter comes
A snowstorm will gather
Over Baoshi Hill
Snowflakes will fall on my balcony
Covering the footprints of Bibi my dog

When winter comes
In a village in the Little Xingan mountains
A boy will climb a freight train
On its way to a faraway town
Looking for a doctor who can help his father

*Lima-Shanghai, 2013*
*trans. Kuo-ch'ing Tu and Robert Backus*

# 冬日的变奏

1  云彩

那些白色的超凡入圣的天物
我曾亲眼看见它们溶化在蓝天里
它们是佛罗里达夏季的一片海滩
是科罗拉多峡谷中的一块崖石
或只是一个躯体让我盲目地坠入

2  音乐

我看见树木与房舍之间
早晨的大海缓慢下来
太阳倾身在空气里捕捉
那无法捕捉到的东西

3  天井

那片闪耀着露珠的绿色草坪
被几条白色的小径分隔
橡树的叶子散落其中
来自阿默斯福特的蒙得里安
从传说的天井里走过

## *Variations on a winter's day*

1 Clouds

Those white supernatural holy bodies
I have seen with my own eyes how they dissolve into the
blue
They are a stretch of summer beach in Florida
a jutting crag in a Colorado canyon
or simply a body that lets me blindly fall in

2 Music

I hear between the trees and the houses
the early morning ocean slowing down
The sun leans into the air to capture
Something that cannot be captured

3 Courtyard

The green lawn sparkling with drops of dew
is divided by a footpath of white sand
the yellow oak leaves fallen there
across the legendary courtyard
have the colour of a Mondrian painting in Amsterdam

4　扇尾鸟

一只过路的扇尾鸟栖息在屋顶上
轻捷的脚步，美丽无比的羽毛
又一个夜晚潜伏在我的身后
她凝望着我庄严神圣犹如
碧空凝望着大海，大海凝望着月影

5　女子

长长的指甲之夜
一双被风吹散了的眼睛
我在你的鼻梁上
发现了火奴鲁鲁

*1993，弗雷斯诺*

4 Fantailed bird

A passing long-tailed bird rests on the roof
steps lightly with feathers of incomparable beauty
Another night, hidden behind me
She gazed at me solemn and sacred
like an emerald sky gazing at the ocean
while the ocean gazes at the moon's shadow


5 A girl

A night of long fingernails
a pair of eyes blown away by the wind
atop the bridge of your nose
I discover Hawaii

*Fresno, 1993*

# VI
# The heart of a poet

诗人的心

## 每一片云都有它的名字

飞机穿越厚厚的云层
上下颠簸左右摇晃
时间无穷无尽地延伸

既然我们选择了天空
就应该把自己的身体献出
每一片云都有它的名字

我们可以把它们描画出来
标出大小和相互间的距离
再添上四种不同的颜色

我们的未来之路也是如此
天空有多么辽阔
人生就有多么曲折

2013,洛杉矶-上海

## *Every cloud has its own name*

The plane passes through thick clouds
Shakes up and down, left and right
Into the time extending endlessly

Since we have chosen the sky
We should sacrifice our bodies
Because every cloud has its own name

We can map the clouds
Measure the distance between them
And paint them four different colors

Our future is like that
The hardships of life
Are as infinite as the sky

*Los Angeles-Shanghai, 2013*

### *诗歌来源于担忧*

当一场暴风雪即将来临
　而没有来临

当一件事故即将发生
　而没有发生

当你心仪的人即将离去
　而没有离去

当一次旅行即将结束
　而终于结束

*2006，圣彼得堡*

## *Poems are born from anxiety*

When a storm is coming
    but never comes

When an accident's about to happen
    but never happens

When the one you love is leaving
    but never leaves

When a journey is about to end
    then finally ends

*St Petersburg, 2016*

## 诗人的心

一片些微的亮光突然
在乌云密布的天空出现
给湖水添加了一丝蓝色

诗人的心也理应如此
拨开忧愁的迷雾之后
在黑暗中打开一扇窗子

*2007，拉芬尼*

## *The heart of a poet*

a glimmer of light appears suddenly
in the darkly clouded sky
giving the lake a bluish tinge.

the heart of a poet should be like this.
after pushing aside the fog of sadness,
it opens a window in the dark.

*Lavigny, 2007*

## 时间之书

如同整数有单数和双数之分
书籍有正面和反面之别
时间也被切割成白昼和黑夜

可是,当我翻动书页
最末一行和最初一行
并未有明显的差异

这便是黄昏的奇异之处
还有早晨,时间之书的智慧
尽在其中,奥妙无穷

*2007,拉芬尼*

## *The book of time*

like numbers are divided into odd and even,
a book has its front and back,
and time is cut into day and night.

but when I turn the pages over,
there is no obvious difference
between the first and the last line.

this is the uniqueness of twilight,
and also of dawn – the profound
and subtle nature of the book of time.

*Lavigny, 2007*

## 墓地

比起宅第和居室来
它更需要鲜花的装扮
犹如一个待嫁的新娘

没有栅栏或篱笆
就像是一家子人
围坐在庭园的草坪上

只要是风和日丽
总会有鼓手敲击蓝天
总会有迎亲的队伍来

*2007，拉芬尼*

## *Cemetery*

Compared with rooms and houses,
it's in need of flowers for decoration.
like a bride to be soon married

without fence or barrier,
as if all members of the family
are sitting around the lawn in the yard.

as long as it is a fine warm day,
there will be drummers beating the sky,
and a team ready to fetch the bride.

*Lavigny, 2007*

## 心灵

比一片叶子轻
犹似小鸟的歌唱
比一座村庄重
犹似教堂的钟声

写在脸颊上
用一支无形的笔
又时常不可见
隐没在湖水中

*2007，拉芬尼*

## *Soul*

Lighter than a leaf
like the song of a bird —
heavier than a village
or the ringing of church-bells.

It writes on the cheek
with an invisible pen —
and often it hides
in the water of a lake.

*Lavigny, 2007*

## 死亡

那么多死亡压迫在我们身上
像一座座巍峨宽广的大山
压迫在我们柔软的身体上
年复一年,代复一代

那么多死亡幻化为海水
承载着大小不一的船只和命运
将躯体凿成灯火通明的隧道
连接着迷惘的昨日和今天

那么多死亡开成了花朵
装点着我们的苦难和生活
让天空布满祈祷的蜡烛
带给我们慰藉和虚幻的憧憬

那么多死亡变成了泥土
长出了庄稼,铺就了道路
那么多死亡与我们相互依偎
陪伴我们走向各自的明天

*2016,洛杉矶-上海*

## *Deaths*

So many deaths oppress us
As if a range of wide towering mountains
Has been pressing down on our soft bodies
Year after year, generation after generation

So many deaths changed into sea water
Carrying different sized ships, different fates
Carving bodies into tunnels with lights
Which connect today to lost yesterdays

So many deaths blooming into flowers
Decorating our lives and our suffering
Let the sky be full of prayer-candles
Bringing us comfort and illusions

So many deaths turned into mud
to grow crops in, or to surface roads
So many deaths so close to us
Travelling with each of us into our futures

*Los Angeles-Shanghai, 2016*

## 为高铁事故遇难者而作

盛夏南国的夜晚
你们悬挂在空中
人数疑似不详

就在一刻钟以前
你们途经我的故乡
停歇了一分钟

前方又将迎来隧道
在一片油菜地上方
天空出奇的宁静

你们就要跨越瓯江
那条孩提时代
我心目中的大河

去到远方的一座城市
不曾料想,倏忽之间
已抵达人生的终点

2011,杭州

## Tribute to the victims

*After the Wenzhou Bullet Train disaster, June 2011*

On a midsummer eve in the southlands,
You were suspended in the air,
How many you were, as yet unclear.

Just a quarter-hour before,
You passed through my homeland,
Stopping for one brief minute.

Another tunnel beckons up ahead,
Above a field of canola
The unusual quiet of the sky.

You were crossing the River Ou,
The great river of my mind's eye
When I was a child.

Travelling to a far-off city,
Unwittingly, instantly,
You reached the end of life's journey.

*Hangzhou, 2011*
*trans. Duncan James Poupard*

## 雪 崩

他们厌倦了房屋和街道厌
倦了绿色和湖水
进入到一片耀眼的白色

他们想要在这里头
安置一个属于自己的家那
里没有沙发、书和汽车

他们骑着黑蓝的雪橇选择
一个晴好无风的日子溜进
了这片白色

*2007，拉芬尼*

## *Avalanche*

they were tired of houses and streets,
tired of the colour green and lake-water —
they entered into the dazzling white.

they wanted to stay here,
set down their own home —
where there were no sofas, books or cars.

they rode on a blue-black sled
choosing a fine windless day,
and slipped into this expanse of white.

*Lavigny, 2007*

## 差异

河流诞生于
崇山峻岭之中
而平整的土地
容易滋养湖泊

人类的思想
也受制于经历
有的深邃
有的开阔

*2007，拉芬尼*

## *Difference*

rivers are born
in steep towering mountains
while flat lands
easily nourish lakes.

so too are people's thoughts constrained
by the terrain of their experiences –
some are deep,
some are wide.

*Lavigny, 2007*

## 天空

我们从未看见过黑夜
看见的只是黑夜中的亮光

天空是大地的必要补充
仅有太阳和月亮远远不够

那样我们甚至无法呼吸
也难以相互交流和信任

天空是我们思想的源泉
是一切虚空的依托和保障

*2013，洛杉矶*

## *The sky*

We never actually see the night
What we see are stars lighting the night sky

The sky is the earth's closest companion
Sun and moon are not enough for us

Without the sky we can't even breathe
Or trust each other or even connect

The sky is the source of all our thoughts
The foundation protecting all emptiness

*Los Angeles, 2013*

# VIII
# Song of the Quiet Life

## 幽居之歌

## 1 天使的早点

预言家的嘴
幻想的前额

赤裸的人们相爱
异己的玻璃托盘

触摸之吻
黄色覆盖了一切

心的空寂
马匹的嘶鸣

## 1  Angel's breakfast

The mouths of prophets
The foreheads of fantasy

Naked people fall in love with each other
Someone else's glass fruitbowl

The kiss and the touch
Yellow covering everything

The deserted heart
The whinnying of horses

## 2 怀念肖邦

数个世纪的梦
开始雕刻一张脸

落叶和岁月的歌
在自身以外扎下了根

溺死的少女的眼睛
遗失在水的记忆中

贞节无形的花
开在沉默的昏黄之茎上

## 2  Missing Chopin

Over several centuries
dreams begin to carve a face

A song of fallen leaves and years
has taken root outside itself

The eyes of a drowned little girl
are lost in the memory of water

Chaste like an invisible flower
opening silently on a pale yellow stem

## 3　歌

赤足的光芒
落叶的簌簌之声

昆虫的衣饰
车轮的欢愉之歌

波浪破碎
使我们陷入白色

一个世界堕落
犹如游牧部落的母亲

## 3  *Song*

Dazzling bare feet
rustle over dry leaves

The garments of insects
The happy song of bicycle wheels

A wave breaks
we fall into the white surf

The world degenerates
like the mother of a nomadic tribe

## 4 万事万物

卧室里盛开着玫瑰
地面上散落着苹果

电话铃声不断响彻
在手臂和脚踝之上

一只年轻羚羊的血
在月亮的公园里闪烁

没有眉头的鱼跳跃
在我隐秘的身体近旁

## 4  Everything

In the bedroom the rose is in full bloom
On the ground scattered apples

An unanswered telephone
sounds over bare arms and ankles

A young antelope's blood
glitters in a moonlit park

A fish without eyebrows leaps
next to my hidden body

## 5　骚动的树木

火焰的跃动，星辰的闪射
可以看作布道

暖风轻拂着白云
时间的重量在增加

巨石在阳光中显现
碎裂成片断

使一列行进的火车倾覆
奉献出多具死尸

## 5  Anxious trees

The leaping of flames, the shooting of stars
can be seen as small sermons

A warm wind lightly strokes the clouds
the weight of time is on the increase

A huge rock appears in the sunlight
breaks into pieces

overturning a train
leaving many dead bodies

## 6　开花的骨头

在我的身后
土地簇拥着

秋天来到,转眼间
桂花的香气弥漫

一位少女俯身
捧着我的脸庞

她稚嫩的小手
渗出了鲜血

## 6  Flowering bones

The earth covers me
pressing on all sides

When autumn comes
sweet osmanthus fills the air

A young girl bends down
lifts up my face

Her delicate hands
are lacerated

## 7　微小的卧室

一部书：一片海洋
负载了多少文字的小船

雄鹰般的眼睛巡视着
捕捉这个或那个单词

拱门，桥梁，黄玉之塔
珠宝，尸衣，矮小的麦束

挑逗性欲的粼粼水波
在幽暗的天花板上流淌

## 7  Small bedroom

A book is like a small sea
bearing many boats of words

The eye patrols like a bird of prey
ready to seize this word or that

An arched entrance, a bridge, a yellow tower,
jewellery, the clothes of a corpse, a wheat shoot

Clear waves enticing passions
flow over the dark ceiling

## 8 午后的生命

午后一阵突来的风
在蔚蓝的天空飘忽

围绕着自身翻转
在流水的催促之下

它避开飞鸟的眼睛
选择了僻静的居所

而死亡犹如深厚的土地
承受了人类所有的过错

## 8  Life after noon

The wind comes suddenly after noon
gusting through a deep blue sky

turning and tumbling over and over
at the urging of running water

It avoids the eyes of birds in flight
chooses a secluded place to settle

But death is like the deep earth
which tolerates all human errors

## 9　多手之躯

它占据了硕大的空间
而我到过更远的地方

一片叶子：一只小手
沐浴了阳光、空气和水

我用手指拧下它的手指
另一只稚嫩的手迅速成长

多么粗壮挺拔的躯体啊
有谁能够从心灵上靠近

## 9  *Body with many hands*

It occupies a gigantic space
but I have travelled further

A piece of leaf like a small hand
that has bathed the sunlight the air and the rain

I use my finger to twist its finger
another delicate hand quickly grows

How straight and sturdy its body is
but who can approach its mind

## 10　乱石的岁月

赏心悦目的秋天
脱衣在水上

瞬息逝去的美
像飘坠的月光

带刺的星星和树叶
飞满了天空

巨大无边的沙漠
唯一的石块在淌血

## 10  *Years of scattered stones*

It is a pleasant autumn
Someone is taking off her clothes by the water

A beautiful moment
which shimmers like falling moonlight

Leaves and thorny stars
fly up filling the sky

In the vast boundless desert
a solitary stone is bleeding

## 11　潮湿的沉默

世界向一颗栎树倾斜
走近，迈着下午的脚步

秋天的上衣宽松整洁
发梢微微弯向河岸

而白露在青草上闪耀
跳动着少女的心

用她那眼睛的叶片
遮住了星星的话语

## 11  Wet silence

The world tilts towards an oak tree
comes closer, walking in the footsteps of the afternoon

The coat of autumn is loose and clean
its hair bends slightly to the riverbank

White dew sparkles on the grass
and a young girl's heart is beating

She has blocked the words of the stars
with the leaves of her eyelids

## 12　伸长的躯体

当我越过栎树之巅
望见光溜溜的山崖
落叶在身后发出笑声

我生来就在树上
我的身躯是你的两倍
手臂在夜晚更加洁白

一场春雨把赤足浇灌
密封的姓名缠绕着枝条
束缚之水向前奔流

## 12   Elongated body

Peering over the top of the oak tree
I see the smooth cliff
while fallen leaves laugh behind me

I was born to live in trees
my stature is twice yours
my arms are whiter at night

A spring rain conceals my bare feet
A concealed name twines round a branch
the water flows rapidly forward

## 13 夜

夜封住了她的唇
玉米的唇

夜分开了她的腿
杏仁的腿

夜深入她的躯体
香蒲的躯体

夜来到这个世界
谁能够避而不见

## 13  Night

The night has sealed up her lips
lips of corn

The night has opened her legs
legs of almond

The night has penetrated her body
body of reeds

Who can avoid it
Night has come to our world

## 14　黑暗的果实

我把舌头伸向世界
随处可闻苹果的芳香

剥了皮的香蕉在腐烂
红红的柑桔把核吐弃

李子树从夜的怀抱里醒来
探出许多白色的脑袋

这是一个梦游的时刻
多少贪婪的嘴张开着

## 14  Dark fruit

I extend my tongue into the world
everywhere smell the fragrance of apples

The skinned banana is rotten
spit out the pips of the red orange

The plum tree wakes from the bosom of night
stretches out many white heads

This is the time for dreaming
how many greedy mouths open

## 15　*鱼*

只有刺秩序井然
陌生的日子和水

鳞片的呢喃
夜与波浪纠缠一起

尾鳍挨着尾鳍
犹如时光的守护者

充满渴意的嘴唇
吸下了又一口空气

## 15  Fish

The fishbones are perfectly symmetrical
strange days and water

Their scales twitter
the night and the waves intertwine

Tail next to tail
like the guardians of time

The lips feel thirsty
swallow more air

## 16　月亮的桥

月亮的桥通向马萨诸塞
通向窗外的一片桉树叶

月亮的桥穿越厚厚的墙
返回到词语的家园

月亮的桥闭上冰冷之唇
忍受着太阳的早泄和不育的痛苦

丧失记忆的黑暗的双乳
为我们竖立了不朽的丰碑

月亮的桥通向眉头和子宫
弥补了这个世界的空虚和不足

## 16  Bridge of the Moon

The bridge of the moon reaches all the way to Massachusetts
to a tuart leaf outside a window

The bridge of the moon passes through a thick wall
turning back to the homeland of words

The bridge of the moon closes ice-cold lips
and endures the sun's premature ejaculation

Two breasts lose their memory in the darkness
stand erect like a timeless milestone

The bridge of the moon links the forehead and the womb
and fills up the insufficiency of this world

## 17　已经迟了

骑马穿过夜晚
语词在那里堆砌

处女的血和眼泪
无休止地坠落

太阳的脸，湖泊的脸
变成了腐朽的面具

水晶之柳，水的白杨
一柱被风吹散的喷泉

## 17  Already too late

I ride a horse through the night
where words pile up

A virgin's blood and tears
drop endlessly

The sun's face, the lake's face
turn into decayed masks

A willow tree of crystal, a white poplar of water
the column of a fountain blown away by the wind

## 18　幽居之歌

花瓣零落犹如钟声鸣响
还有印度墨水、银纸、涂色纸

纯净的眼睛和睫毛
随处可见时间的碎片

从身躯之外伸出一只手
触摸了已故明星的下颚

一只小鸟在梦中尖叫
灰色之夜的又一次显现

*1992，杭州*

## 18  Song of the quiet life

The petals fall like bells ringing
Indian ink, silver paper, paper to paint on

Pure eyes and eyelashes
everywhere the fragrance of time

Stretching out my hand
I touch the filmstar on the calendar

A bird screams in my dream
the grey night returns again

*Hangzhou, 1992*

Appendix
# Essays

附录
散文二篇

# West Lake, or Five Instants of Dream

by Cai Tianxin
translated by Robert Berold and Huang Jiaju

1

### At the water's edge

*Dusk approaches. Thousands of cold crows*
*Gather above the lake. The temperature drops*
*To the top of a nearby hill. The setting sun in the west*
*Vanishes in the shrubbery.*

*At the water's edge, I sing in a low voice,*
*Imagine splashing the water with my tongue*
*Until stars appear in the words of my song*
*And run down lines of tears.*

One afternoon in the early spring of 1991, I sat alone idly beside West Lake and wrote, or rather received, this poem. This murmuring is a portrait of my youth. That day was overcast, quiet and ordinary. I left my room in the single teachers' residence by bike, rode through the gate, and on towards Children's Palace along Xixi Road and Baochu Road. I quickened my speed to the right, rode up Broken Bridge, then pedalled slowly along Baidi Causeway. It was a time when I enjoyed roaming between words and things, indulging in the pleasure of naming things. Hangzhou was a small city then, and life was simple. There were few places to relax in, neither bars nor teahouses nor discos. There were no private cars, deluxe apartments or fivestar hotels. The society was not yet cleanly divided into blue collar and white collar, rich and poor.

Though Baidi Causeway was not far from downtown, I seldom met anyone I knew there. Most tourists were from out of town, which made the place seem illusory. Besides, I hadn't been living in Hangzhou that long, so I had a different feeling each time I wandered around West Lake. If I had not been so greedy, looking to West Lake so often for inspiration, I would have learnt something from my riding and rambling. As the French philosopher Gaston Bachelard put it "At some moments of a poet's life, imagination assimilates reality." However, the poems I wrote had nothing to do with West Lake or the city of Hangzhou. Yet that afternoon was somehow unusual. I strolled up and down Baidi Causeway and finally settled on a bench, gazing at the chilly lake. Only as darkness fell, and I glanced back to look at Baoshi Hill, did I find inspiration for a poem. That experience was wonderful beyond words, in the same way that, this very moment, imagination draws its pictures from memory. What was especially rare and precious was that it was a poem about West Lake.

# 2

My home town lies on the coast of the East China Sea, a place fertile in oranges and loquats, in a county that no longer exists as an official unit. I was born and grew up there, and did not leave that area until I entered university. The first time I heard about West Lake must have been just before I was nine years old. In that year Richard Nixon, the president of United States, visited Beijing for the first time, then came to Hangzhou. When newspapers published photos of the American guests viewing fish at Flower Harbor, the beauty of West Lake became imprinted deeply on my heart. I can still remember now on the wall of the county bus station, the sign saying: 324 kilometers to Hangzhou, ticket price 7.8 Yuan. But whenever I took the bus, it was to Wenzhou or somewhere nearer. Only six years later did I get the opportunity to see West Lake and the city nestled beside it with my own eyes. You can hardly imagine what that first glimpse meant for a boy who loved dreaming.

I saw West Lake on the way to my university in Jinan, which was also my first long distance journey. When the bus crossed Qiantang River Bridge, the first things I saw were the Six Harmony Pagoda and the memorial museum for Cai Yongxiang. Only the memorial appeared in our middle school textbook then, not the pagoda – even its thousandth anniversary was neglected. This sounds incredible, it would be seen now as a waste of a business opportunity. To tell the truth, I still doubt whether the incident known as "class enemies sabotaging the bridge" ever actually happened. If it did, they were indeed real terrorists. Along the shady Nanshan Road to the north, West Lake flashed by in the distance fulfilling a childhood dream. This kind of epiphany happened again only seventeen years later, on the Eurostar Express from Nice to Paris.

The key sites of interest of Jinan included Baotu Spring and Daming Lake, the only lake in the northern cities comparable with the Summer Palace in Beijing. The couplet on Xiaocanglang Pavilion says "four sides of lotuses and three sides of willows, a city of mountain and half a city of lake". Tu Fu's poem "this pavilion west of the sea is old, Jinan has many personalities" brought great fame to this city of springs. One of the eight literary masters of Tang and Song dynasties, Zeng Gong, had once been the governor of Jinan. The former residences of two great poets of the Song Dynasty, Li Qingzhao and Xin Qiji, are situated near the lake and the spring. The novelist of the late Qing Dynasty, Liu E, in his masterpiece Travels of Lao Can, described Daming Lake beautifully in the opening chapter. Nevertheless, none of these had moved me. It was on my way home in the winter and summer vacations that I lingered on in Hangzhou and left the footprints of my first love beside West Lake. At that time I was concentrating on roaming the kingdom of mathematics. Years later, after I got my final degree, I came to Hangzhou as a teacher, and wrote a poem as a memory of my adolescence. It was also one of my earliest writings on West Lake.

### *Baoshi Hill*

*The leaves of willows ripple above West Lake*

*alternating one peach, one willow*

*with the peach trees in blossom*

*Towards the west of Broken Bridge*

*lovers crowd like raindrops*

*towards the west*


*It is February, early spring*

*on the abundant green of Baoshi Hill*

*whose lips open and speak?*

# 3

"Paradise is above, Suzhou and Hangzhou below". The origins of this old saying seem impossible to trace now. It has a geometrical imagination not surpassed by the Tang poet Bai Juyi's "recall Jiangnan, recall Hangzhou most" (Jiangnan being the areas south of the Yantze Rive) – the poet's recollection on the prime of life. Nor is it surpassed by the Song poet Su Dongpo's "comparing West Lake to Xi Zi / a famous beauty of ancient times/ her makeup is always appropriate" – his recollection of youth gone by. The thirteenth century Venetian Marco Polo's perception was "Suzhou is the city of earth, as Hangzhou is the city of heaven." In his famous Travels this great traveller devoted fourteen whole pages to Hangzhou, and only one to Suzhou. He used the phrase "heaven on earth" (which is now the name of a bar near West Lake). The description in The Travels of "the world's most solemn and beautiful city" and its inhabitants remains quite accurate for Hangzhou even today. He described its citizens as being fond of eating quails, poultry and seafood luxurious weddings and banquets, paintings and interior decoration, and the city as having, among others, an astonishing number of prostitutes, handsome men, and warmhearted women.

I don't know when the beautiful landscape of West Lake began to become more static and fade, even a means to stifle literary talents. Many gifted poets and writers lost their imagination and daring too early for this reason. Lu Xun once wrote a poem to dissuade Yu Dafu from moving his home to Hangzhou. His comment on West Lake was: "as for the scenery of West Lake, it is pleasant, there are plenty of places to eat and play, but if it is indulged in, the views of lake and mountain will wear down one's ambition." This kind of perception is not only held by literary people. From Shaoxing, the hometown of Lu Xun, eastward to Ningbo, people seem to admire the lifestyle and rhythm of Shanghai. That's why Hangzhou Bay Bridge, a bridge directly connecting Ningbo and Shanghai (and avoiding the longer route via Hangzhou) was put on the agenda. In the early 1950s, the then mayor of Shanghai, Marshal Chen Yi, visited Hangzhou. The top officials of Zhejiang province feted him and asked him to compose a few words of commemoration or instruction. Unexpectedly humorous, Chen Yi quipped "The city leaders of Hangzhou are traditionally good at poetry, how come the mayor has no verse now?" This embarrassed the hosts. Indeed, after Su Dongpo, which city official of Hangzhou could be proud of his literary ability? After Su Xiaoxiao, women striking both in literature and beauty have also been difficult to find, so that the amorous Zhejiang poet Xu Zhimo had to move his love elsewhere.

Elizabeth Bishop wrote "Is it lack of imagination that makes us come to imagined places, not just stay at home?" "Home is the place to start from" is the opening sentence of a short piece of prose I wrote. Perhaps it is strange – after all, I lived in Hangzhou, heaven on earth. After my student journeys to the northwest, northeast and southwest, in the first three summers of the 1990s I visited three coastal cities –

Fuzhou, Qingdao and Xiamen. Obviously, the blue sea elicits fantasy. The boundless water can not only absorb the dreams of childhood, but also soothes the wounded soul. Xiamen University (possibly the most beautiful university in China) gave me inspiration. Its campus is not only near the beach, it also has a pleasant little lake, on which one can row a boat the whole day and the whole night. I recorded that journey with a short poem. It was also the first time I fell in love with a lake which was not West Lake. Maybe I saw it as an extension of West Lake.

### *Lotus Lake*

*Once while rowing on Lotus Lake, I saw*
*a young woman deep in thought on the shore*
*the buttons glinting on her summer dress.*
*Rowing closer, I invited her to join me.*

*At first I startled her, but then she smiled.*
*Twilight fell around us, shortening*
*all distances ; a subtle beauty spot*
*closer than a book, further than a star*

# 4

Marco Polo's Travels provoked in the west an endless fascination for the east. At the same time it stimulated my own dreams to travel to the west. After a brief visit to Hong Kong in the fall of 1993, I hurried to the United States of America. Its exotic views, people, and customs were like a fresh breeze on my face, and unlocked every pore of mine to breathe freely. In a short time I wrote dozens of poems. Many of them , like Niagara Falls, Yosemite and Millerton Lake (which lies in the San Joaquin Valley of the west coast) express my feeling about beautiful scenery although they lack historical depth.  I also wrote a poem on my way back through Japan titled Lake Ashi, which lies in the embrace of Hakone Mountains in the middle of Honshu. However these feelings contained no specific regional flavour. Even after I befriended the vast mist-covered Lake Michigan in Chicago and Lake Ontario in Toronto, my poems still transmitted a flavour of the east.

### *Lake water*

*The land is an expanse of lake water*
*The sky is an expanse of lake water*
*The city is an expanse of lake water*
*The house is an expanse of lake water*

*The wall is vertical lake water*
*The chair is folded lake water*
*The teacup is lake water rolled up*

*The towel is hanging lake water*

*Sunshine is transparent lake water*
*Music is flowing lake water*
*Love is mutual-feeling lake water*
*The dream is imaginary lake water*

"No land pleases me: that's the kind of traveller I am" said French poet Henri Michaux in his Ecuador. His first two poetry collections were both about imaginary journeys. In fact, travelling is a universal need of human beings, a means to extend the content of our lives. I have always believed that a real poet or artist need not necessarily be knowledgeable, but he has to have the need to breathe fresh air. As Arthur Rimbaud wrote, "Life is elsewhere". The students of Paris University daubed this on the walls of their campus. Milan Kundera used "Life is elsewhere" as the title of a novel. In it he writes: "Just like the sisters of Rimbaud's mentor Izambard – those famous lice-catchers – went to the French poet, after his long time of roaming, seeking them for shelter. They bathed him, cleansed him of dirt, and purged him of lice." The travels of a poet are full of freedom, ecstasy and solitude.

Every time I returned to Hangzhou from a foreign land, I had new discoveries and perceptions about the city. I wrote lines like "Her beauty injected mild venom into my body" ... "I have my two oars: words and imagination" ... "The luxurious serenity and the ambitious simplicity reflect each other". Not only that, it gave me a pretext and opportunity for a new literary form – prose. The use of the internet is supposed to make the physical location of the writer less important, for example the writing of scientific papers. The only vital thing is supposed to be the writer's frame of mind. However that is not my own experience. In my literary production I have only been able to write prose at home and poems abroad. My trip around the Mediterranean, especially the new millennium trip to Latin America and the journey from the Dead Sea to the Caspian Sea, made me savor again the welling up of poetic inspiration. All the way, I heard Michaux's voice "I write to you from a distant land".

## 5

Hangzhou is the city I have lived in longest, and my observation of this city is also the most detailed. More than any other tourist site in China, West Lake is like a landscape painting, condensed from generations of writers' and poets' ideals of beauty. In fact, many people encounter Hangzhou for the first time through the paintings on folding fans, which predestines it to be a compact 'folded' city. Although it is growing in scale and population, it is only after midnight that the lakefront area of Sixth Park and Nanshan Road exhibits any light and vitality. Different from Yellow Mountain, Lijiang River, Great Wall or the Terracotta Warriors of Xi'an, the beauty of West Lake relies on cultural romance and literary reference. This predestines her fame to be localised only in the Chinese world and those of its neighbours which are influenced by Chinese culture. Unless one day Hangzhou hosts an international poetry festival, inviting the world's best poets as her guests, and some literary giant says something like "Whoever is tired of Hangzhou, is tired of life".

Meanwhile as time goes on I myself feel somewhat distanced and estranged from Hangzhou. Its dialect, which has remained unchanged for thousands of years, sounds like the mother tongue of a fish kingdom, and is always repellant to me. Living on the north side of Baoshi Hill, West Lake seems like the back of a hand pointing towards the bustling passersby, with Baidi Causeway and Sudi Causeway its veins. As time goes by, I have become a tourist of Hangzhou myself. Only that way can I regain my point of view. Sure enough, on one summer day at the end of last century, I found a more abstract expression for West Lake.

### *Lake*

1

*Over the bright clear surface*
*a swallow flies through the sky*

*to this tiny lake*
*it is a fighter plane*

2

*Two wooden paddles swung*
*by a thin old man*

*the wet hull*
*cleaves to the surface*

3

*The lake mirrors the mountains*
*below the deep green wave*

*perhaps there's a tropical forest there*
*where fish and hunters patrol*

4

*A faint cool breeze*
*ripples over the lake*

*the lake has many worries*
*it only appears to be indifferent*

> 5
> 
> *People swarm from the water to the shore*
> *their faces like scales of fish*
> 
> *sunlight cuts like a blade*
> *blocked by thick branches*
> 
> > 6
> 
> *Darkness shrouds us*
> *someone throws in a stone*
> 
> *its sound persists*
> *reverberating*

Perhaps this is my ideal of West Lake, a thing that came to me a long time ago. It can be viewed as public scenery, or like the back of my hand, always with me whether on a bench in Paris, London or New York, or in a jungle in South America, Australia or Africa.

*Hangzhou, 21 August 2002*

# Mathematicians and Poets

by Cai Tianxin
translated by Robert Berold and Gu Ye

Mathematicians and poets exist in our world as uncanny prophets. The difference between them is that poets are thought to be arrogant because they tend to be proud and lonely by nature, while mathematicians are thought to be unapproachable because they exist on a transcendent plane. Thus in literary circles poets are often considered to be socially inferior to novelists in the same way that mathematicians are considered socially inferior to physicists in scientific and technological associations. But these things are only superficial.

"I'm a failed poet," the novelist William Faulkner said humbly in his later years. "Maybe every novelist wants to write poetry first, finds he can't and then tries the short story which is the most demanding form after poetry. And failing at that, only then does he take up novel writing." Physicists, by comparison, are not so modest. Nevertheless, for a physicist every increase in knowledge of physics is always guided in two ways, by mathematical intuition and empirical observation. The art of physics is to design experiments in order to derive the laws of nature. In this process mathematical intuition is indispensable. In fact it is easy for mathematicians to switch to studying physics, computer science or economics, just as it is for poets to turn to writing novels, essays or plays.

Mathematics is usually seen as the diametric opposite of poetry, and although this is not always the case, no one can deny it. Mathematicians work to discover, while poets work to create. The painter Degas occasionally wrote sonnets, and once complained to the poet Mallarmé. He said that he had many ideas, in fact too many, he found it difficult to write. Mallarmé replied, "poems are made not with ideas but with words." On the other hand, mathematicians, especially algebraists, work mainly on concepts, combining concepts of the same kind. In other words, mathematicians think in an abstract way, while poets think in a concrete way. But again this is not always the case.

Both mathematics and poetry are products of imagination. For a pure mathematician, his or her materials are like lacework, leaves on a tree, a patch of grass or the light and shade on a person's face. In other words, "inspiration", which Plato denounced as "a mania of poets," is equally important to mathematicians. For example, Goethe fancied that he saw a flash of light when he heard of his friend Jerusalem's suicide. He immediately came up with the outline of The Sorrows of Young Werther. He recalled that he "seemed to have written the book unconsciously." Another example: Gauss, 'the prince of mathematics' wrote to tell a friend after solving a problem (symbols of Gaussian summation) which had been bothering him for years, "Finally, two days ago, I succeeded – not on account of my hard efforts, but by the grace of the Lord. Like a sudden flash of lightning, the riddle was solved. I am unable to say what the conducting thread was that connected what I previously knew with what made my success possible."

Mathematics often appears to be connected to and interactive with astronomy, physics and other branches of natural science, but it is a completely self-referential and vast field of knowledge with a reality more enduring than other sciences. It is like a true language, which not only records and expresses ideas and the process of thinking, but also creates itself through poets and writers. It could be said that mathematics and poetry are the freest intellectual activities of human beings. The Polish mathematician Paul Turan maintained that "Our mathematics is a strong fortress." His words correspond to Faulkner's "People will never be destroyed as long as they yearn for freedom."

Through years of study and practice, I have come to believe that the process of mathematical research is more or less an exercise of intelligence and the process of its appreciation. This is perhaps one of the main reasons for its great charm. I fully understand what the philosopher George Santayana said in his later years, "If my teachers had begun by telling me that mathematics was pure play with presuppositions, and wholly in the air, I might have become a good mathematician, because I am happy enough in the realm of essence." Of course, I cannot rule out the possibility that a great thinker can yield to the intellectual fashions of his times as a woman can do to fashions in dress.

Compared with any other discipline, mathematics is an undertaking for the young. The Fields Medal, the most renowned mathematical prize, goes only to mathematicians under forty. Riemann died at forty, Pascal at thirty-nine, Ramanujan at thirty-three, Eisenstein at twenty-nine, Abel at twenty-seven, and Galois at twenty; by the time they died they had already established themselves as great mathematicians. Some mathematicians, such as Newton and Gauss, lived long lives, but they completed their major work in their youth. Likewise we can draw up a long list of poets who died young: Pushkin, Lorca and Apollinaire died at thirty-eight, Rimbaud at thirty-seven, Wilde at thirty-four, Mayakovsky at thirty-two, Plath at thirty-one, Shelley and Yesenin at thirty, Novalis at twenty-nine, Keats and Petofi at twenty-six , and Lautreamont at twenty-four. Whereas if we look at painting, Gauguin, Rousseau and Kandinsky began their artistic careers after they turned thirty. Therefore I'm convinced that more than any of the other scientific and artistic disciplines, mathematics and poetry need talent. The difference between them is that poets destroy what their predecessors built, while mathematicians have to build on the achievements of previous generations. Because of this, poets can appear or disappear more easily than mathemati-cians.

The language of poets is renowned for its conciseness. Ezra Pound is praised as a master of the concise; no one seems to do better than him in this regard. But the language of mathemati-cians is also noted for its conciseness. The British writer Jerome K. Jerome gave an example, as follows:

> *When a twelfth-century youth fell in love he did not take three paces backward, gaze into her eyes, and tell her she was too beautiful to live. And if, when he got out, he met a man and broke his head – the other man's head, I mean – then that proved that his – the first fellow's – girl was a pretty girl. But if the other fellow broke his head – not his own, you know, but the other fellow's – the other fellow to the second fellow, that is…*

As he goes on to say, this interminable paragraph would be very succinct if expressed in mathematical symbols:

> *If A broke B's head, then A's girl was a pretty girl; but if B broke A's head, then A's girl wasn't a pretty girl, but B's girl was.*

Not only that, the language of mathematicians is universal. Goethe joked that mathematicians are like the French, who can translate whatever you say into their own language and turn it immediately into something totally new. Marx taught us that a branch of science is truly developed only when it is able to make use of mathematics. In the same way, poetry is a common key factor of all the arts. It can be said that every work of art needs 'poetic flavor'. Mozart had a reputation as 'the poet of music' and Chopin 'the poet of the piano'. It's not difficult to imagine the striking symmetry between a beautiful mathematical formula in a scientific paper and several brilliant lines of poetry in an essay or a speech.

Now let's come back to the proposition stated at the beginning of this essay. Freud said, "Everywhere I go, I find that a poet has been there before me." This remark was taken up by Breton, the leader of surrealism, as a golden rule. Novalis asserted, "Poetry is very similar to prophecy in its significance. Generally, poems are like the intuitions of prophets. Poets – prophets – reveal the secrets of a strange and wondrous world with magic lines and images." Therefore a poet of integrity will inevitably violate the interests of the ruling class. Plato accused poets of being the enemies of truth and their poetry of spreading mental poison. On the other hand, pure mathematics, especially modern mathematics, often develops in advance of its time, even in advance of theoretical physics. It was more than a full century after the invention of Galois's Group Theory and Hamilton's Theory of Quaternions that these theories were applied to quantum mechanics. In similar situations, non-Euclidean geometry was used to describe gravitational fields, and Complex Analysis to describe electrodynamics. The discovery of conic sections, which for over two thousand years was considered no more than "the unprofitable amusement of a speculative brain," ultimately found application in modern astronomy, the theory of projectile motion and the law of universal gravitation.

However more often than not, the work that mathematicians do is not understood. Some people have rebuked them for indulging in pointless speculation or being silly and useless dreamers. Lamentably, this viewpoint of these learned scholars was supported by some authorities. St. Augustine condemned Homer's fabrications as corrupting people's minds, "transferring things human to the gods." "We have no choice but to go astray on the false path of poetry," he said. At the same time, he raged, "Good Christians should beware of mathematicians and all those who make empty prophecies. The danger already exists that the mathematicians have made a covenant with the devil to darken spirits and to confine man in the bonds of Hell." And did not the Roman jurists rule "concerning evil-doers, mathematicians, and the like," that "to learn the art of geometry and to take part in public exercises, an art as damnable as mathematics, are forbidden"? Schopenhauer, a distinguished modern philosopher, acknowledged poetry as the highest art but described arithmetic as the lowest activity of the spirit. Since the beginning of the twentieth century, more and more people have come to realize how our times have benefited from mathematics; at least authorities like St. Augustine are no longer there to disturb us. To some extent, however, poets and artists are still in the situation they always have been. Perhaps they should console themselves with Picasso's words: "People earn the title of artists only after they have overcome innumerable obstacles. Therefore art should be restricted instead of being encouraged."

By coincidence, mathematicians and poets often walk side by side on the frontiers of human civilization. Euclid's Elements and Aristotle's Poetics, the two most important academic works of ancient Greece, were written at almost the same time, and both were based on the imitation of three-dimensional space. The dif-ference is that the former was an abstract imitation while the latter was a concrete one. Edgar Allan Poe and Baudelaire, pioneers of modern art, belonged to the same age as Lobachevsky and Bolyai, founders of non-Euclidian geometry. When a group of poets and painters of great talent gathered in Paris, in the 1930s and 1940s, to launch the radical revolution of surrealism, some other bril-liant minds in the world were working hard in their own way to develop Topology, a burgeoning branch of mathematics. Here I want to quote an example, a story often cited by topologists from The Song of Hiawatha by the American poet Longfellow (written in 1855, Dvorak composed his Symphony No.9 "From the New World" inspired by this poem). The story is about an Indian who made fur mittens:

*He, to get the warm side inside, Put the inside (skin side) outside; He, to get the cold side outside, Put the warm side (fur side) inside...*

The Indian was in fact performing a topologic movement when turning the glove inside out and outside in. Interestingly, the word Topology first appeared as Topologie in German, in the work of a student of Gauss in 1847, when the concept was known to very few mathematicians.

Finally I'm going to raise the question of whether someone can be a poet and a mathematician at the same time. Pascal as-sures us at the beginning of his Pensées: "As long as geometri-cians have good insight, they can be sensitive; as long as sensitive people can apply their insight to geometric principles, they can be geometricians too." Despite this, historically only the 18th century Italian mathematician Mascheroni and the 19th century French mathematician Cauchy could possibly be counted as poets, while the 20th century Chilean poet Parra was a professor of mathematics. Perhaps the only one in human history who made great contributions in both fields was Omar Khayyam, the 11th century Persian who was born four centuries earlier than the versatile Da Vinci. He made his mark in the history of mathematics for his geometric solution of cubic equations; and he became known to the world as the author of the Rubáiyát. When the fourteen-year-old T.S. Eliot came across Edward FitzGerald's English translation of the Rubáiyát at the turn of the 20th century, he immediately became enthralled. He recalled the splendor of entering the world of this magnificent poem and realized, after reading those lines full of "dazzling, sweet and painful colours", that he wanted to be a poet.

*Hangzhou, May 1991*

*Notes*

1 The Hungarian poet Petofi disappeared in a battle against the Russian-Austria alliance in 1849. He was considered to "have died at the points of the lances of Cossack soldiers" until the end of the 19th century, when Russian researchers found in archives that he had actually been taken to Siberia as a prisoner of war and died there of tuberculosis in 1856. He would therefore have been thirty-three when he died.

2 Mr. Plato was always precise in his diction. In his last work he described those who ignored the importance of mathematics in the pursuing of ideals as "piggish".

3 This viewpoint of Schopenhauer is completely contrary to that of Plato, who claimed that he would drive poets out of his ideal city and that "God is a geometrician."

# Afterword

## by Robert Berold

I met Cai Tianxin in South Africa in 2003. I first saw him on the stage of the Poetry Africa Festival in Durban. He had flown for 30 hours to give us a 20 minute reading –poetry is expensive, he said, laughing. Then he read this magical poem:

> *Branches grow from clouds.*
> *Birds fly eagerly towards my eyes.*
>
> *Landscape and smoke billow over the house.*
> *Rivers run along my arms.*
>
> *The moon is a blue sapphire*
> *Set in a ring.*
>
> *I stand on the precipice of the ear*
> *Dream of living in the world.*

Two years later, thanks to Cai, I found myself in Hangzhou, the city the ancient Chinese called 'Heaven on Earth', and which Marco Polo in the thirteenth century described as "the most splendid city in the world". I came there to teach at Zhejiang

University, where Cai is a professor of mathematics. Over twelve weeks we met every Saturday to make this book of English translations – or rather he did rough translations into English and together we 'translated' them into English poems.[1]

We also travelled together – to the fishing town of Shi Pu during the Spring Festival, crossing the Ningbo Strait on a ferry, surrounded by children wearing their brand new clothes. And also to Cai's home town of Huang Yan for a poetry festival hosted by the local writers association : "My home town lies on the coast of the East China Sea, a place fertile in oranges and loquats, in a county that no longer exists as an official unit. I was born and grew up there, and did not leave that area until I entered university...

***    ***    ***    ***

Cai Tianxin's own name comes from a poem. He was born on 3 March 1963 and his father, who knew classical poetry well, chose his name from a poem by Du Fu, which starts on an uncharacteristic note of celebration :

> *On March 3 the weather is new. At*
> *the water's edge of Chang An there*
> *are many beautiful women.*

'Tian' means 'weather' or 'day' and 'xin' means 'new',

---

[1] This process needed much back and forth discussion and dictionary-checking to ensure it reflected the original. All unnamed translations in this book were made by Cai and myself this way, while those of sections V-VII were done via email, with myself and Ma Xiujie working together in South Africa, and Cai in Hangzhou. All other translators are named beneath each poem.

so 'tianxin' can be read as 'fine weather' but also as 'every day new'. This is not far from Pound's Confucian-inspired dictum 'make it new'. Incidentally, 'Chang An' is the ancient name of Xi'an, in the Tang dynasty the capital of China.

Tianxin's father, Cai Hainan, was a high school headmaster who had studied history at Beijing University and taught himself English. In the Cultural Revolution, like many people with any education, he was branded a rightist and sent to do manual labour in the countryside. He herded livestock and worked as a cook and became highly skilled in carpentry. Tianxin completed school just as the 'great chaos' was coming to an end and academic standards were being restored. His father insisted he study sciences, because he felt it was an occupation that couldn't be politically compromised.

Cai specialised in mathematics and grew to appreciate the inner world that it presented to him. In an essay titled 'Mathematicians and Poets' he wrote "Mathematics is a true language, which not only records and expresses ideas and the process of thinking, but also creates itself (through its own poets and writers). It could be said that mathematics and poetry are the freest intellectual activities of human beings." He continues "A poet of integrity will inevitably violate the interests of the ruling class" and quotes Novalis : "Generally, poems are like the intuitions of prophets. Poets – prophets – reveal the secrets of a strange and wondrous world with magic lines and images."

\*\*\* \*\*\* \*\*\* \*\*\*

Every Cloud Has Its Own Name shimmers with changes of image and perspective, both peaceful and disturbed, like fragments of classical poetry cut up and re-assembled.

Part I of the book is made up of relatively straightforward poems in which the poet establishes his particular kind of emotional geometry.

Part II groups poems about love and desire and poetry, which fuse into an 'erotics of poetry':

> *At first I startled her, but then she smiled.*
> *Twilight fell around us, shortening*
> *all distances ; a subtle beauty spot closer than*
> *a book, further than a star*

Parts III IV and V consists of poems written while travelling, to countries as far-flung as Russia, Switzerland, India, and North and South America. Cai could literally be the most travelled person in all of China, having visited over a hundred countries. In his childhood, hemmed in by mountains and lack of money, he never travelled anywhere: "I can still remember now on the wall of the county bus station, the sign which read: '324 kilometers to Hangzhou, ticket price 7.8 Yuan'. But whenever I took the bus, I could only afford to go to Wenzhou or somewhere nearer. When I finally saw West Lake and the city nestled beside it with my own eyes… you can hardly imagine what that first glimpse meant for a boy who loved dreaming."

Cai's travels are always both outer and inner journeys, which lifts them out of the tourist mould. He is fascinated by changes of perspective. In his poem about the ancient Peruvian city of Cuzco, he says

> *The city shows off its unique beauty*
> *in its squares, stone arches*
> *and elongated roof tiles*
>
> *At night there is laughter from the balcony The*
> *lamp above is like an eyebrow*
> *A full moon rises over the reeds*

The ancient architecture – squares, arches, rectangles – are juxtaposed with the eyebrow-shaped lamp; as are the laughter in the moment alongside the full moon so ever-present in Chinese poetry: the ephemeral and the eternal, the near and the far.

The poem 'Distant Places' describes how the disjunction of perspective sparks the poetry:

Part VI brings the poems home – poems distinctly about China and Hangzhou, together with more personal feelings and memories. This is followed by Part VII, which reflects more deeply on the mind's refractions and transformations:

> *I'm always attracted by distant places, Always*
> *attracted by floating scenery –*
> *Only when the bird circles the rice-field, Do I*
> *notice its golden colour.*
> *Only when the wind blows over*
> *And rattles the peach-tree by my side,*
> *Do I find the shadow of its branches graceful.*

> We never actually see the night
> What we see are stars lighting the night sky
> 
> *("The Sky")*
> 
> So many deaths changed into sea water Carrying
> different sized ships, different fates Carving bodies
> into tunnels with lights Which connect today to
> lost yesterdays
> 
> *("Deaths")*

The final section, Part VIII, 'Song of the Quiet Life', is an extraordinary 18 poem sequence written in a burst of inspiration on a single day in 1992. It is an entire small universe of space, feeling, and sensuality:

> The petals fall like bells ringing
> Indian ink, silver paper, paper to paint on
>
> Pure eyes and eyelashes
> everywhere the fragrance of time

The reader of Every Cloud Has Its Own Name travels and dreams with the poet into a freshly imagined world: "I have always believed that a real poet or artist need not necessarily be knowledgeable, but he has to have the need to breathe fresh air... The travels of a poet are full of feedom, ecstasy and solitude."

*Grahamstown, South Africa*
*April 2017*

# 西湖，或梦想的五个瞬间

## 一

### 在水边

黄昏来临，犹如十万只寒鸦，
在湖上翻飞；而气温下降，
到附近的山头，像西沉的落日
消失在灌木丛中。

我独自低吟浅唱，在水边。
用舌头轻拍水面，溅击浪花。
直到星星出现，在歌词中，
潸然泪下。

  1991年初春的一个下午，我独自一人闲坐西子湖边，写下或者说是得到了这首诗，这段喃喃低语成了我青年时代的一段生活写照。记得那天天色阴沉沉的，一个寂寥平凡的日子，我离开校内的单身宿舍，骑车出了大学校门，沿着西溪路和保俶路来到少年宫。接着，向右加速并冲上了断桥，然后沿着白堤缓缓骑行。那会儿我喜欢在词与物之间徜徉，陶醉于为事物命名的幸福之中。那会儿杭州还是一座小城市，人们的生活比较单纯，既少有酒吧、茶馆、迪厅之类供人消遣娱乐的地方，也没有私家轿车、高级公寓甚或五星级酒店。换句话说，社会阶层还没有明显地分化出蓝领和白领、穷人和富人。

白堤虽然离开闹市区不远，却难得碰到一个熟人，大多数游客都是外地人，这容易营造出一种幻景。加上那时我到杭州的时间不长，每次逛西湖都有不一样的感觉，假如我不那么贪心，不经常到湖边寻觅灵感，我总能在骑车或漫步途中有所斩获。如同哲学家加斯东·巴拉什所说的，"在诗人生活的某些时刻，梦想将现实本身同化了。"不过，我写的诗歌与西湖甚或杭州这座城市没有什么关系。可是，那天下午却多少有点反常，我在白堤上来回转悠，最后竟然在一张长椅上坐了下来，呆呆地望着冷飕飕的湖面。直到黄昏来临，我回眸凝望宝石山的那一瞬间，才似乎发现了什么。那种体验妙不可言，就像此时此刻，想象力的作用使得记忆栩栩如生，同时也为记忆绘制出插图。殊为难得并值得珍惜的是，这是一首关于西湖的诗。

## 二

我的故乡在东海之滨，一个盛产蜜橘和枇杷的地方，一个消失了的县级行政单位，我在那里出生、长大，直到考上大学。我第一次听说西湖必定是在九岁以前，因为那年的残冬和初春之交，美国总统理查德·尼克松首次访问了北京，接着他来到杭州。当报上登出客人们在花港观鱼的照片时，西湖的美丽已经深深地印刻在我的心上。至今我依然记得，县城汽车站的墙壁上写着：到杭州的里程324公里，票价7元8角。可是，每回我都是去温州或更近的地方，直到六年以后，我才得以亲眼见到西湖和那座依偎在她身边的城市。人们无法想象，那最初的一瞥对于一个喜欢梦想的男孩来说意味着什么呢？

我是在去济南上大学的路上见到西湖的，那也是我第一次出门远行。当汽车从茅以升的钱塘江大桥上穿过，我首先看到的是六和塔和蔡永祥纪念馆，当时出现在中学教科书上的只有那座纪念馆，并没有江南名胜六和塔，甚至于连建塔一千周年也被忽略而过，现在想起来简直不可思议，那不是明摆着的错失商机吗？说句老实话，我现在怀疑，当年是否真有"阶级敌人破坏大桥"这件事？那样的话可是名副其实的恐怖分子了。沿着绿树成荫的南山路向北，西子湖若隐若现，童年时代的一个美梦实现了。那种感受惟有在十七年以后，我乘坐高速火车从尼斯去往巴黎的旅途中才失而复得。

济南的名胜中有趵突泉和大明湖，后者是北方城市里惟一可以与颐和园相媲美的湖泊，小沧浪亭的楹联"四面荷花三面柳，一城山色半城湖"和杜甫的诗句"海右此亭古，济南名士多"使得泉城名声大震。"唐宋八大家"之一的曾巩做过济南太守，宋代两位大词人李清照和辛弃疾的故居也坐落在湖畔泉边，清末小说家刘鹗的名作《老残游记》开篇就把大明湖写得挺美的。可是，这一切均未能打动我，倒是好多次寒暑假期间，我回家路上滞留杭州，并把初恋的足印留在了西子湖畔。那时候我正潜心在数学王国里遨游，若干年以后，我取得最后的学位来到杭州任教，才写下一首诗，作为青春期的一个纪念，那也是我最早点名西湖风景的作品之一。

### 宝石山

柳丝漂漾在湖上
被一簇簇桃花
分隔

断桥向西
雨点一样密集的情侣
向西

> 早春二月
> 青郁的宝石山上
> 是谁的嘴唇开口说话？

## 三

  古谚云，"上有天堂，下有苏杭"，其出处恐怕已无从考证了。这句话有着"几何学的想象力"，比起唐代诗人白居易的"江南忆，最忆是杭州"（老年对壮年的回忆），或者宋代词人苏东坡的"欲把西湖比西子，浓装淡抹总相宜"（对逝去的青春的缅怀）来，一点也不显逊色。对此，十三世纪的威尼斯人马可·波罗有着自己的理解，"苏州是地上的城市，正如京师是天上的城市。"这位大旅行家对京师（杭州）情有独钟，在那部影响历史进程的游记里，他花费了整整十四页的篇幅（苏州只占一个页码），还使用了"人间天堂"这个词，如今已成为西湖边上一家酒吧的名字。即使在今天看来，这部游记对当时"世界上最庄严秀丽的城市"及其居民的描述仍十分准确，例如喜欢吃鹌鹑、家禽和海鲜，向往奢华的婚礼和宴席，爱好绘画和室内装修，妓女的数量多得惊人，男人的清秀和对女人的体贴，等等。

  不知从何时开始，西湖美丽的风景在我眼里逐渐凝固和淡化，甚至成为扼杀才华的一种手段和工具，许多天资聪颖的诗人和作家过早地丧失了想象力和进取心。当年的鲁迅就曾写诗劝阻郁达夫把家迁往杭州，他对西湖的概括性评价是："至于西湖风景，虽然宜人，有吃的地方，也有玩的地方，如果流连忘返，湖光山色，也会消磨人的志气。"这样的观点绝非文人所独有，从鲁迅故乡绍兴向东直到宁波，人们似乎更崇尚沪上的生活方式和节奏，以至于直接连接宁波和上海的杭州湾大桥被提上议事日程 。

上个世纪五十年代初，时任上海市长的陈毅元帅到杭州巡游，浙江省的头儿们设宴接风，并请他题词，不料生性幽默的陈毅脱口而出，"杭州知府例能诗，市长今日岂无词？"令主人颇为尴尬。的确如此，苏东坡之后，还有哪一任杭州的父母官恃才自傲呢？苏小小之后，才貌双全的佳人也难觅，以至于近水楼台的多情才子徐志摩只好移恋别处。

"是因为缺少想象力才使我们离家/ 远行，来到这个梦一样的地方？"（伊丽莎白·毕晓普的诗句），继学生时代游历了西北、东北和西南以后，我在九十年代的头三个夏天，先后去了三座海滨城市——福州、青岛和厦门。"家是出发的地方"，这是我一篇短文的开头一句，其意义非同寻常，因为我住在天上人间的杭州。显而易见，蓝色的大海更诱使人想入非非，那无边无际的水域既可以接纳童年的美梦，又能够抚慰受伤的心灵。厦门大学（可能是中国最美丽的大学了）带给我灵感，校园不仅紧挨着海水浴场，还有一个小巧可人的湖泊，居然可以通宵划船。我用一首小诗记录了那次旅行，那也是我第一次倾心于西湖以外的湖水，或许，我把它看成了西湖之水的一种延伸，

### 芙蓉湖

一次我驾舟在芙蓉湖上
一位少女在岸边沉入遐思
她夏装的扣眼里闪烁着微光
我驶近她，向她发出邀请

她惊讶，继而露出了笑容
暮色来到我们中间，缩短了
万物的距离，一颗隐微的痣
比书籍亲近，比星辰遥远

## 四

　　马可·波罗的旅行激发了西方人对东方无穷无尽的向往，同时也反过来让我们产生了西游的梦想。1993年秋天，在对香港进行了一次短促的访问之后，我匆匆踏上了美利坚合众国的土地。异国的景色、人物和风俗如春风扑面而来，我开启身上的每一个毛孔呼吸，很快写出了一百多首诗歌，其中不乏对秀美却缺乏历史沉淀的风景的情感抒发，例如《尼加拉瓜瀑布》、《约塞米蒂》和《米勒顿湖》，后者位于西海岸的圣瓦莱山谷，以及归途游东瀛所获的《芦之湖》（坐落在本州中部箱根群山的怀抱之中）。可是，这类情感通常不带有任何鲜明的地方色彩，即使在芝加哥（多伦多）亲近了烟波浩淼的密执安湖（安大略湖）以后，下面这首诗仍然透射出一股东方韵味：

　　　　湖　水

　　　大地是一片湖水
　　　天空是一片湖水
　　　城市是一片湖水
　　　房屋是一片湖水

　　　墙壁是垂立的湖水
　　　椅子是折叠的湖水
　　　茶杯是卷曲的湖水
　　　毛巾是悬挂的湖水

　　　阳光是透明的湖水
　　　音乐是流动的湖水

爱情是感觉的湖水
梦忆是虚幻的湖水

"没有一个地方让我喜欢：我就是这样的旅行者。"法国诗人亨利·米肖在《厄瓜多尔》(1929)里这样写到，他最早的两部诗集都是关于想象中的旅行的书。其实，旅行是人类的普遍需要，也是延扩生命内涵的有效方式。我一直以为，真正的诗人和艺术家未必要见多识广，可他需要时常呼吸鲜活的空气。如同阿瑟·兰波的诗中所写的："生活在别处"，巴黎大学的学生曾把这句话刷写在校园的墙壁上，米兰·昆德拉用它命名了一部小说，其中提到："就像兰波的老师伊泽蒙巴德的妹妹们——那些著名的捉虱女人——俯向这位法国诗人，当他长时间地漫游之后，便去她们那里寻求避难，她们为他洗澡，去掉他身上的污垢，除去他身上的虱子。"诗人之旅，是享尽了自由、孤独和极乐的精神之旅。

而我每次异国漫游以后回到杭州，总能对这座城市有新的发现或感受，"她的美丽在我身上注射了一枚温和的毒汁"，"我有我的双桨：语词和梦想"，"奢华的宁静和追名逐利的纯朴交相辉映"。不仅如此，我还为自己找到借口和契机来从事一种新的文学形式——散文的写作。本来，英特网的使用使得写作地点变得不那么重要（就像科学论文的写作一样），惟一重要的就是一个人的心态。可是，这种事说起来容易做起来难，有很长一段时间，我的文学创作交织着两种状态：在国内写散文，在国外写诗歌。而环地中海之旅，尤其是新千年的拉丁美洲之行和从死海到里海的旅程，则让我再次体验到诗歌灵感的喷发，一路行走，我都听见了米肖的声音，"我从遥远的地方为你们写作。"

# 五

然而，杭州这座城市毕竟是我居住得最久的，我对她的观察也较为细致。比起中国任何一处风景来，西湖更像一幅山水画，浓缩了一代代文人墨客的理想之美。事实上，有许多人都是在折扇上第一次认识她的，这一点注定让杭州成为一座袖珍型的城市，尽管她的规模和人口日渐庞大，可是一旦过了子夜时分，惟有六公园到南山路的湖滨一带尚余几处亮光和喧嚣。与黄山、漓江、长城、秦始皇兵马俑这些奇异的景观不同，西湖之美依赖于人文的渲染和典故，这注定了她的知名度局限于汉语世界和受华夏文化影响较深的邻国。除非有一天，杭州主办国际诗歌节，邀请世界各国的顶尖诗人来做客，某位大文豪说出"谁厌倦了杭州，谁就厌倦了生活"之类的话，不胫而走。

与此同时，随着时间的推移，我本人对杭州也有了某种隔膜或疏离，它的千年不变的方言，听起来像是鱼类王国的母语，始终为我所排斥。居住在宝石山的北侧，西湖对于我就像是一只手背，总是朝向熙熙攘攘的行人，而白堤、苏堤便成了手背上流淌的血脉。久而久之，我自己也成了杭州的一名游客，惟其如此，我才有可能再次获得观察的角度。果然，在上个世纪末的一个夏日，我为西湖找到了一种较为抽象的表现方式。

湖

1

明亮清澈的水面
燕子在天空飞翔

对于小小的湖泊
它就是一架歼击机

2

两支木桨摇响
一个瘦瘦的老家伙

滋润的船体
委身于湖面

3

青山倒映在湖中
那碧绿的水波下

可有烈炎的森林
鱼儿和猎人一起巡游

4

一阵微弱的凉风吹过
湖上漾起了层层涟漪

湖水的心事重重
徒有冷漠的外表

5

一大群人爬上了岸
他们的面孔像鱼鳞

阳光似刀片切割下来
被茂密的树枝遮拦

6

黑夜来到我们的周围
有人扔下一块石子

可以听见一种声音
在湖上久久地回荡

或许，这就是我心目中的西湖，她只是由来已久的一件事物。既可以被看作一处公共景点，又像是我的一只手背，可以随时跟我去到巴座丛林中。

2002年8月21日，杭州

# 数学家与诗人①

数学家和诗人都是作为先知先觉的预言家存在我们的世界上。只不过诗人由于天性孤傲被认为狂妄自大，而数学家由于超凡脱俗为人们敬而远之。因此在文学艺术团体里诗人往往受制于小说家，正如在科学技术协会里物理学家领导数学家一样。但这只是表面现象。

"我做不了诗人"，晚年的威廉·福克纳彬彬有礼地承认，"或许每一位长篇小说家最初都想写诗，发觉自己写不来，就尝试写短篇小说，这是除诗以外要求最高的艺术形式。再写不成的话，只有写长篇小说了。"相比之下，物理学家并不那么谦虚，但无论如何，对每一个物理学家来说，物理认识的增长总是受到数学直觉和经验观察的双重指导。物理学家的艺术就是选择他的材料并用来为自然规划一幅蓝图，在这个过程中，数学直觉是不可或缺的。一个不争的事实是，数学家改行搞物理学，计算机或经济学，就像诗人转而写小说，随笔或剧本一样相对容易。

数学通常被认为是与诗歌绝对相反的，这一点并不完全正确，可是无可否认，它有这种倾向。数学家的工作是发现，而诗人的工作是创造。画家德加有时也写十四行诗，有一次他和诗人马拉美谈话时诉苦说，他发现写作很难，尽管他有许多概念，实际上是概念过剩。马拉美回答：诗是词的产物，而不是概念的产物。另一方面，数学家主要搞概念，即把一定类型的概念组合起来。换句话说，数学家运用了抽象的思维，而诗人的思维方式较为形象，但这同样不是绝对的。

数学和诗歌都是想像的产物。对一位纯粹数学家来说，他面临的材料好像是花边，好像是一棵树的叶子，好像是一片青草地或一个人脸上的明暗变化。也就是说，被柏拉图斥为"诗人的狂热"的"灵感"对数学家一样的重要。举例来说，当歌德听到耶路撒冷自杀的消息时，仿佛突然间见到一道光在眼前闪过，立刻他就把《少年维特之烦恼》一书的纲要想好，他回忆说："这部小册子好像是在无意识中写成的。"而当"数学王子"高斯解决了一个困扰他多年的问题（高斯和符号）之后写信给友人说："最后只是几天以前，成功了（我想说，不是由于我苦苦的探索，而是由于上帝的恩惠），就像是闪电轰击的一刹那，这个谜解开了；我以前的知识，我最后一次尝试的方法以及成功的原因，这三者究竟是如何联系起来的，我自己也未能理出头绪来。"

数学虽然经常以与天文、物理及其它自然科学分支相互联系、相互作用的方式出现，但从本质上说，它是一个完全自成体系的（对它本身来说又是极为宽广的）、最具有真实性的知识领域。这一点正如真正的文字语言，它不仅用来记载和表达思想及思维过程，并且反过来（通过诗人和文学家）又把它们创造出来。可以说数学和诗歌是人类最自由的两项智力活动。匈牙利数学家保尔·图拉认为：数学是一座坚固的堡垒。这应验了福克纳的话：人只要有向往自由的意志，就不会被毁灭。

通过多年的研究实践，我认为数学研究的过程或多或少是一种智力的锤炼和欣赏的过程，这或许是数学研究之所以有如此吸引力的一个重要原因。我非常能够理解哲学家乔治·桑塔耶纳晚年说过的一席话："如果我的老师们真的曾在当初就告诉我，数学是一种摆弄假设的纯粹游戏，并且是完全悬在空中的，我倒可能已经成为优秀的数学家了。因为我在本质王国里感到十分幸福。"当然，在此我不能排除伟大的思想家追求时代智力风尚，就如同妇女在服饰上赶时髦一样。

与任何其它学科相比，数学更加是年轻人的事业。最著名的数学奖——菲尔兹奖是专门奖给四十岁以下的数学家的。黎曼死于四十岁，帕斯卡尔死于三十九岁，拉曼纽扬死于三十三岁，艾森斯坦死于二十九岁，阿贝尔死于二十七岁，伽罗华死于二十岁，而他们作为伟大数学家的地位却已经奠定。有些数学家虽然长寿，但他们的主要工作大多是在青年时代完成的，例如牛顿和高斯。另一方面，我们可以开列一长串早逝的诗人名单：普希金、洛尔迦和阿波利奈尔死于三十八岁，兰波和顾城死于三十七岁，王尔德死于三十四岁，马雅可夫斯基死于三十二岁，普拉斯死于三十一岁，雪莱和叶塞宁死于三十岁，诺瓦利斯死于二十九岁，李贺、济慈和裴多菲死于二十六岁[②]，洛特雷阿蒙死于二十四岁。而以绘画为例，高更、卢梭和康定斯基都是三十岁以后才开始艺术生涯。因此，我们有理由认为，在科学、艺术领域里，数学家和诗人是最需要天才的。不同的是，对诗人来说，一代人要推倒另一代人所修筑的东西，一个人所树立的另一个人要加以摧毁。而对数学家来说，每一代人都能在旧建筑上增添一层楼。由于这一原因，诗人比数学家更容易出现或消失。

诗人的语言以简练著称，埃兹拉·庞德被誉为"简练的大师"。这方面似乎没有人做得更好，殊不知数学家的语言也是如此，英国作家J·K·杰罗姆曾举过一个例子，有这样一段描写：

> 当一个十二世纪的小伙子坠入情网时，他不会后退三步，看着心爱的姑娘的眼睛，他说她是世界上最漂亮的人儿。如果他在外面碰上一个人，并且打破了他的脑袋——我指的是另一个人的脑袋——那就证明了他的——前面那个小伙子的——姑娘是个漂亮的姑娘。如果是另外一个人打破了他的脑袋——不是他自己的，你知道，而是另外那个人的——对后面那个小伙子来说的另外一个——那就说明了……

倘若我们把这段没完没了的叙述借助数学家的符号表达出来，就变得非常简洁明了：

> 如果A打破了B的脑袋，那么A的姑娘是个漂亮的姑娘。但如果B打破了A的头，那么A的姑娘就不是个漂亮的姑娘，而B的姑娘就是一个漂亮的姑娘。

不仅如此，数学家的语言还是一种万能的语言，歌德曾逗趣说："数学家就像法国人一样，无论你说什么，他们都能把它翻译成自己的语言，并且立刻成为全新的东西。"马克思更是教导我们："一门科学只有当它达到了能够运用数学时，才算真正发展了。"与此相应，诗是一切艺术的共同要素，可以说每一件艺术品都需要有"诗意"。因此，莫扎特才有"音乐家诗人"的美誉，而肖邦也被称为"钢琴诗人"。不难想像，在一篇科学论文中出现一个优美的数学公式和在一篇文章或谈话中间摘引几行漂亮的诗句，两者有一种惊人的对称。

现在让我们回到本文开头提出的命题。佛洛依德认为："诗人在心灵的认知方面是我们的大师。"这句话曾被超现实主义领袖布勒东奉为圭臬。诺瓦利斯声称："诗歌的意义和预言十分相似，一般来说，和先知的直觉差不多。诗人——预言家通过有魔力的词句和形象使人得以触及一个陌生而神奇的世界的奥秘。"因此，一个正直的诗人难免会冒犯统治阶级的利益。柏拉图历数诗人的两大罪状：艺术不真实，不能给人真理；艺术伤风败俗，惑乱人心[③]。另一方面，纯粹数学尤其是现代数学的发展往往是超越时代的，甚至是超越理论物理学的。例如，伽罗华群和哈密尔顿四元数的理论在建立一个多世纪以后才开始应用于量子力学；非欧几何学被用来描述引力场、复分析在电气动力学中的应用也有类似的情况；而圆锥曲线自被发现二千多年来，一直被认为不过是富于思辩头脑中的无利可图的娱乐，可是最终它却在近代天文学、仿射运动理论和万有引力定律中发挥了作用。

然而，更多的时候，数学家的工作仍不被人们理解。有这样的指责，认为数学家喜欢沉湎于毫无意义的臆测，或者认为数学家们是笨拙和毫无用处的梦想家。可悲的是，这些饱学之士的观点还得到某些权威的支持。圣奥古斯丁一面攻击荷马的虚构败坏人心，"把人间的罪行移到神的身上"，"我们不得不踏着诗的虚构的足迹走入迷途"，一面又叫嚷道："好的基督徒应该提防数学家和那些空头许诺的人，这样的危险业已存在，数学家们已经与魔鬼签订了协约，要使精神进入黑暗，把人投入地狱。"古罗马法官则裁决"对于作恶者、数学家诸如此类的人"，禁止他们"学习几何技艺和参加当众运算数学这样可恶的学问"。叔本华，一位在现代哲学史上占有重要地位的哲学家，一方面视诗歌为最高艺术，另一方面却把算术看成是最低级的精神活动④。进入二十世纪以来，越来越多的人认识到了，我们这个时代是如何受惠于数学的，至少奥古斯丁那样的权威人士销声匿迹了。但是诗人和艺术家的境况在某种意义上依然如故，或许他们应该用毕加索的话来聊以自慰：人们只有越过无数障碍之后，才能得以登上艺术家的宝座。因而对艺术非但不该加以鼓励，相反应压抑它。

数学家和诗人常常是不约而同地走在人类文明的前沿。古希腊最重要的两部学术著作——欧几里得的《原本》和亚里士多德的《诗学》几乎诞生在同一时代，并且都是建立在对三维空间摹仿的基础上。只不过前者是抽象的摹仿，后者是形象的摹仿。现代艺术的先驱爱伦·坡、波德莱尔与非欧几何学的创始人罗巴切夫斯基、鲍耶也属于同一时代。本世纪三、四十年代，当一批才华横溢的诗人、画家聚集巴黎，发动一场载歌载舞的超现实主义革命时，这个世界上另一些聪明绝顶的头脑正各自为营，致力于发展新兴的数学分支——拓扑学。这里我想引用一个拓扑学家经常引用的例子，美国诗人朗费罗的长篇叙事诗《海华沙之歌》（作于1855年，德沃夏克的《自新大陆交响曲》即受其影响写成）中有一段故事，讲到一个做毛皮手套的印第安人：

>他把晒暖的一侧弄到里面，把里面的皮翻到外面；
>把冷冰冰的一侧翻到外面，把晒暖的一侧弄到里面……

在手套的翻进翻出过程中，这个印第安人实际上是在做一个拓扑动作。有趣的是，拓扑这个词最早是以德文的形式（Topologie）出现在1847年高斯的一个学生写的著作里，在那个年代拓扑概念只存在极少数几个数学家的头脑里。

最后我要谈到的是，一个人能不能既成为诗人又成为数学家呢？帕斯卡尔在《思想录》开头差不多这样轻松地写道：凡是几何学家只要有良好的洞见力，就会是敏感的；而敏感的人若能把自己的洞见力运用到几何学原则上去，也会成为几何学家。虽然如此，从历史上看，只有十八世纪意大利数学家马斯凯罗尼和十九世纪法国数学家柯西勉强算得上诗人，二十世纪智利诗人帕拉和法国诗人鲁波也曾做过数学教授。而人类历史上惟一能够在两方面都有杰出贡献的或许惟有欧玛尔·海亚姆了，这位十一世纪的波斯人比多才多艺的达·芬奇还早出生四百年，他的名字不仅因给出三次方程的几何解载入数学史册，同时又作为《鲁拜集》一书的作者闻名于世。上个世纪初，十四岁的T·S·艾略特偶然读到爱德华·菲尔茨杰拉德的英译本《鲁拜集》，立刻就被迷住了。他后来回忆说，当他进入到这光辉灿烂的诗歌之中，那情形"简直美极了"，自从读了这些充满"璀璨、甜蜜、痛苦色彩的"诗行以后，便明白了自己要成为一名诗人。

1991年5月，杭州

注释：

① 此文英译文发表在《美国数学会通讯》2011年第4期，斯拉夫译文发表在波斯尼亚和黑塞哥维那的《文学》2009年第7期，土耳其译文发表在《科学与未来》2008年第6期。

②1849年，匈牙利诗人裴多菲在反抗俄奥联军的战斗中失踪，此后一个多世纪一直被认为"死在哥萨克士兵的矛尖上"。近年有档案揭示他作为战俘被押送西伯利亚，1856年死于肺结核。因此他去世时应为三十三岁。

③柏拉图先生的用词向来较有特色，在他的最后一篇著作里，他把那些无视数学对于探求理想的重要性的人形容为"猪一般"。

④叔本华的这个观点正好与柏拉图唱反调，柏拉图声言要把诗人赶出他的"理想国"，同时又称"上帝是几何学家"。

# 后记

## 漫 游

### 蔡天新

我在五色的人海里漫游
林间溪流中飘零的一片草叶

一切都是水，一切都是水
时间自身的船体掉过头来

顺着它蜿蜒的航线而下
一座白柱子的宅第耸立在河岸

斑鸠的飞翔划破了天空的宁静
远处已是一片泛紫色的群山

多年以前，我在加利福尼亚的一次旅途中写下了这首诗，她是我成年以后生活状态的一种呈现，另一种是沉思。我认为，这也是每一位阅读者的两种可能的生活状态。也因为如此，我主编了两本对称的诗集《漫游之诗》和《冥想之诗》（人民文学出版社，2016），约请九位诗人兼翻译家共同注释完成。

2003年5月，正当"非典"在华夏大地施虐之际，我应"非洲诗歌节"组委会的邀请，搭乘如今尽人皆知的"马航"班机，经停吉隆坡前往约翰内斯堡。在浦东机场登机时，我们接受了严格的安全和卫生检查。机上乘客稀少，相邻两三个位置均是空座，几乎每一位都戴着白口罩。到达吉隆坡机场时，又被红外线检测体温。直至飞抵约翰内斯堡，我仍担心会被南非海关拒之门外。

在那次旅行三年以前，我曾有过更为大胆的冒险之旅——只身前往南美洲安第斯山中名城麦德林，在那里的最高学府执教一年。那座哥伦比亚第二大城市是死亡之谷的代名词，既是大毒枭的老巢，又是游击队的活动据点。可我却安然无恙，教学、研究之余，我在那里学会了西班牙语，还受邀参加了名闻遐迩的麦德林诗歌节，结识了世界各国的诗人，这才有了南非之旅。

抵达印度洋最大的港市德班，前来接机的当地诗人们献上热情的拥抱，这让我受宠若惊。原来，南非是艾滋病发病率和死亡率最高的国度，传说中的中国"非典"对他（她）们来说根本算不了什么。

我认识了南非诗人罗伯特·贝洛尔德，他是学院派的典型代表，毕业于剑桥大学，曾在加州大学伯克利分校攻读比较文学博士。后来，罗伯特就像英国大诗人T. S. 艾略特一样，为了写作的理想放弃了学术生涯。难以置信的是，一年以后，罗伯特接受我任教的浙江大学外语学院的邀请，以一个外教的身份来到西子湖畔。

接下来那一年的许多时光，我们在一起交流诗艺、广交朋友，有时也会驱车出游，到达了我的两个故乡。其中有三个月，每个周末我们聚集在一块，翻译我的诗作。期间我才得知，罗伯特在南非还拥有一家叫"远南"（deep south）的出版社。

冒险的事不仅美丽，且总会有所收获。在造访南非三年之际，我的英汉双语诗集《幽居之歌》问世了，封面用了罗伯特喜欢的吴冠中先生的一幅抽象画，为此我特意电话吴老并征得他的同意。正如2002年，在我离开南美大陆一年以后，我的西汉双语诗集《古之裸》由安第基奥大学出版社推出。《幽居之歌》出版以后，从未谋面的南非诗人、批评家加利·库姆米斯基发表了一篇书评《我们在世界的海洋上游泳》（恰好是我法文版诗集的书名），文中写道：

"从某种层面上看，蔡的写作遵循的是中国古典诗歌的传统——诗行中充溢了自然的景象，诸如：湖泊、沙砾、风、花、云、鸟——但诗中明显又有当代的意识流贯穿其间，并经常呈现超现实的意象……"

"在蔡的诗歌中，'二分法'是一个值得注意的叙述特点：他的诗经常从客体转移到主体，从明到暗，从欣喜到痛苦，从欢笑到流泪。尽管许多诗歌的表面十分宁静，底下却时常暗流涌动……"

"这部诗集表面上简洁朴素，其实另有深意；它们总是在暗示某种更为深沉的东西。这些丰富的意象，通常都来自于简洁的词句，正是这些简洁的词句，创造出了一幅幅细致入微的画面来……"

承蒙刘雁女士和壹嘉出版社的鼓励，我和罗伯特修订了这本诗集。我们不仅改换了书名，也添加了三小辑诗歌，即V辑美洲、VI辑远和近、VII辑诗人的心，32首诗歌分别作于北美、南美、瑞士、俄国、印度、中国。除了罗伯特以外，还有几位译者，他们的名字出现在扉页上，分别来自美国、印度、爱尔兰和中国。

除了诗歌以外，本集子还收录了两则随笔，即《数学家与诗人》和《西湖，或梦想的五个瞬间》，前者曾被译成六七种语言并发表，这次作为附录；后者用作代序。这两篇文章是罗伯特与他在浙大任教时的学生合作翻译的，在此表达我诚挚的谢意。

最后，我希望英文和中文的读者朋友能喜欢这些诗和散文。

*2017年5月，杭州*

Every Cloud Has Its Own Name

每片云都有它的名字

Copyright ©2017 by Cai Tianxin

ISBN-10: 0-9985199-6-0
ISBN-13: 978-0-9985199-6-8

All Rights Reserved

1 Plus Books is an independent publisher based in San Francisco Bay Area. We dedicate to publishing high quality fiction and non fiction books in both English and Chinese. For more information, please visit our website:

www.1plusbooks.com.

Phone: (510)248-4244

Email: 1plus@1plusbooks.com

www.ingramcontent.com/pod-product-compliance
Lightning Source LLC
Chambersburg PA
CBHW021120300426
44113CB00006B/231